Chapter One:

The red flag fluttered precariously over the tiny turret of Castle Hamlet. It was a small inoffensive little place, surely the King wouldn't begrudge George this little citadel? Some people couldn't understand why the King hadn't done him in years ago, he seemed to be such a rebel, the lone voice shouting against the system. He railed against the bullies and the killers, but after a time the humans began to look like pigs and the pigs human.

In the distance the Thames merged with the sea in a mass of grey mud, it was from there that most of the villagers of Castle Hamlet had come from, they were dark and swarthy looking little like East Saxons, or any kind of Saxon for that matter. As the wind whipped up they all waited to see the red banner ripped from it's pole and carried over the mud.

"If Allah wills it he will come back to us," one bearded man mused, "Allah protects him."

"Nonsense," another argued, "he is a *kafir*, why would Allah watch over him?"

"Because he does Allah's will," the first man replied.

"No he is just using us," the second grunted.

"There's a carriage!" The village hag declared, she had been here since before the time when the Easterners had come, the East Saxons had all left little by little and now she was one of the few who remained, in a village where she hardly knew anyone anymore.

"It might be the King's men," another dark figure replied, "come to slit all our throats open because of George and all his talk of Cromwell."

"Yes that's not him," another agreed, "he has been thrown in the Tower, no doubt fed to the menagerie there!"

"No it's just one carriage," the hag replied, "the King would send many."

"Yes because he knows he would have a fight on his hands if he came here," the first man argued.

The hag let out a long cackle, "don't you think that the King could drive us all into the river if he wanted to, he has thousands of men under his command? If he wanted to get rid of us do you really think you lot would stop him?"

"Then why doesn't he then?" The first man argued.

The hag shrugged, "that I do not know, if I would have been him I would have done it years ago, but he allows George to carry on talking, there must be some reason to it all but I am buggered if I know." Her eyes then shifted onto a blond haired man who stood out against the tanned faces of the others, their eyes met and she nodded, "God save the King," she smiled, she knew a spy when she saw one.

Then a figure leant out of the carriage almost carried away by the wind gushing past him, "it's Brother George!" It was him! Waving like a conquering hero. It was not far from the small hamlet at the mouth of Old Father Thames to the Mother of all Parliaments, but it was as if he had returned from a dangerous jungle.

"Yes it's George!" Another declared.

As the carriage got nearer they could hear what he was shouting, "they failed! They tried to stitch me up but they failed!" The carriage went over a bump and he went staggering back, only to throw himself at the window again, "they failed!"

"So he's back then," the hag grunted. "It's been quiet down here without him."

The carriage then span round the bend and skidded to a halt, then nothing happened until suddenly the carriage door was flung open and then nothing happened again, a couple of men edged forwards before George emerged, unfurling his opera cape and lashing off his garish hat complete with ostrich feather: "They tried to stitch me up, and they failed!"

A cheer rang up from the crowd, until a sly faced man replied: "They will try again."

George paused, he was nearly fifty but his blue eyes still twinkled as they met the man's, "then they will fail," he then looked over the peasants before shouting, "again!" They cheered and the sly faced man backed away, his hand reaching inside his coat and settling on the cold ivory handle of his dagger, incase the crowd turned on him. George had in fact done very little for this place, it was as poor and neglected as when he had arrived here, but he was their hero because he had stood up to the evil Prince Anthony, but what had they gained through that?

The blond haired man then stepped forwards, "so what do you plan to do now my lord?"

"Lord? I am no lord, I am the same as you!" George insisted.

The hag scratched her head, "doesn't he talk funny?"

"He's a Taffy," someone replied.

"No it isn't Taffy," the hag replied, 'we had a Taffy here some forty summers ago, a right bastard he was, a right proper bastard!" She affirmed loud enough for George to glance towards her.

"I will continue now with my fight against this unnecessary, brutal and," George searched for another word, "bastard!"

The old hag almost fell over with shock.

"It's a bastard war! Damned you Prince Tony! Damned you to hell!" He then waved his fist above him as if battling an invisible demon.

The crowd roared with delight

The old smile returned to his face, the old George smile, "now you all remember how I was against the dictator Mabbus Hassan from the start?!"

The old hag frowned, " I thought that you went over there and said how much you liked him, you admired his courage and his fearlessness."

"No, no, sister, I was not talking about Hassan I was talking about the Mesopotamian people," he then gave her one of those feline smiles and it seemed that her memory was wrong, she scratched her head, as if that would make her brain work again. "No I have always been against Hassan, since his war against the Persians!"

After the scratching the hag's brain seemed to work again, "oh yes that's right George so you were." But still she swore she could remember him stood in front of Hassan who smiled at his kind words. "I was against him when the colonists were sending muskets and crossbows to him to help him against the Persians!" The more George spoke the more it felt like her brain was being cleansed and these silly thoughts no longer had a place there, of course George and Hassan had never been friends. "But I will say one thing life in Mesopotamia was better under Hassan than it is now, our presence there is only making things worse!"

"We can't pull out now!" The blond man shouted. "the whole country would sink into chaos."

"It's in chaos now!" George gasped, "it's in chaos now!"

One of the darker figures nodded towards the blond man, "who is he anyway? He doesn't look like he's from around here."

The old hag sat down, "oh George you have given me a head ache with your talk of Persians and Mesopotamians, I thought that you went to parliament to talk about Castle Hamlet, not these wild places beyond the clouds. I mean what does it matter to us what goes on over there?"

"It matters sister," George became a little tetchy, "because this war is being fought in our name."

"It ain't being fought in my name, none of them foreigners over there who the hell I am."

"You're English aren't you?" George rounded.

"Yes, I suppose so."

"Then the war is being fought in your name!" George rounded on her.

"Maybe so, but why does it bother the rest of you? I'm the only English person left in Castle Hamlet!" The hag protested.

At that even George laughed.

The sly faced man tried to edge back out through the crowd, he had heard enough, the hag's eyes then settled on him, "where's he going?"

"Who is he anyway?"

The fear in the sly faced man's eyes betrayed him, "he's one of the Prince's spies!" Someone shouted.

"And the blondie!" The hag shouted, "him as well, I ain't seen a blondie here for seven summers at least! He ain't from around here," then she drew back and realized in fact that she was the only person who had been born here.

George laughed at first, he always relished a cockfight, the bloodier the better, then as he saw a pitchfork rise up from the crowd panic shot through him, anything that happened here would be blamed on him. "Now come on brothers, we are not like the prince!"

The crowd stopped for a moment before the old hag looked at the crowd with an eye which was like marble, "in the cut with them," she nodded towards the Thames, "a good soaking never did anyone any harm."

"I can't swim!" The sly faced man cried.

"Well you should have learnt," the hag replied.

The black smith's banana like fingers gripped the sly faced man's shoulders, "they'll enter the river dead first!"

George by then had fought his way to the sly faced man's side, "come on brothers we must not stoop to the Prince's ways!"

"It's been a long time since we had a good hanging," one man shouted.

"Burning's better," the hag snapped, "my father said that burning was always the best way, like they did to Guy Fawkes, I mean you didn't hear no more of him after that did you?"

"No," George shouted, "these are the Prince's men, come on comrades, -er I mean brothers and sisters. If anything happens here the Prince will send his men and they will kill every man, woman and child here, then they will dig up the dead to torture them, to see if they know anything. They will burn the place down until it is just ruins, and then they will smash the ruins until they are just dust. When they have finished there won't a turnip growing in the fields because they'll pull it up and cast it into the fire! They will kill every dog, cat and budgerigar!"

"What's one of them?!" The old hag snapped.

"It's a type of bird," George continued, he then carried on with a speech and the crowd seemed to be like a sea whose waves he controlled like King Canute, his blue eyes glinted.

It was a long way to Castle Hamlet from where he had come from in the hard Scottish streets where he had learnt to fight or rather to avoid fighting. George had always been small, smaller than all those around him, and so he kept his mouth shut. His grandfather had always told him never to venture out on Saturdays, because in Dundee Saturday was fight day. There was always a match, of what passed for football in Scotland and after the match there was usually a fight. One Saturday when George was barely ten he had nipped out, and headed towards where he could hear the shouting, slowly he edged forwards and then he saw a field where something had been pulled down and nothing built in it's place. Gingerly he edged forwards as if towards a nightmare, cautiously peering into it, he watched one man on the ground, he was out of the fight but still he was getting kicked by two others so that he wouldn't join the fight again next week. He took some blows to the head before his friends rescued him and started beating the hell out of his two attackers, so that then it was their turn on the floor. There seemed little logic to it, only that one side wore blue and the other orange. George could feel himself shaking and so he drew back, until he backed into someone, he turned round to see a group of teenagers grinning:

"So who do we have here?"

"George Dumfries Sir," George replied.

The fourteen year old leader grinned, "you look about eight."

"I'm ten Sir," George replied.

"Never mind that Tangerine or Blue?"

George smiled, "sorry."

"Tangerine are you?"

George backed away, "I'll have one if you have one."

The fourteen year old grinned, "you're lying, you're a blue."

"No," George stammered, "I like tangerines."

"He doesn't know what we are talking about," one of the others chipped in.

The leader's eyes sank into George's, he wanted to give someone a beating and this little one was just fine, "no I say he's a blue!"

As they moved forwards George backed away, he waited for the other one to say 'no leave him' but he kept silent, he saw all their fists tighten then George stepped forwards and threw back his shoulders, "how dare you! How dare you say that I am a blue!'

The fourteen year old's eyebrows rose and he stepped back.

"I am a tangerine, I have never had anything to do with that blue scum across town! My father is a tangerine and his father was, how dare you say that, I hate them to the pit if my stomach," George felt a power surge through him as someone bigger and stronger bent to his will. "Now instead of us talking let's get them!" George cried and then lead the group running towards the battle, the older boys quickly over took him and George stopped and looked as the fourteen year old threw himself at a thirty year old and clung onto his back, before being hurled to the floor and beaten, he would be lucky to reach thirty himself. For a moment he carried on watching, all the hate, all the anger just over a colour. Imagine if all that fury could be harnessed, imagine the gang he would march across town with, he would own Dundee. That day he had learnt the power of words, the boy who had wanted to beat him was now getting beaten up just because of a few words from George's mouth. George then drew back before running. He ran all the way back to his grandfather's house, the old man was waiting at the door:

"You went out didn't you son?"

"Yes I did grandfather."

"I told you not to but still you did."

"Yes grandfather." George's head bowed.

"I should beat you for that, but tell me George what did you see?"

"There is a field of bricks and rubble and there a group of people wearing orange fought a group of people wearing blue," George stepped forwards, "grandfather which colour are we?"

"Green," the old man replied, looking him in the eye firmly.

George tried again, "but grandfather which side are we on grandfather?"

His grandfather walked over and settled his hand on his shoulder, "we are on neither side George," he then pulled off a green scarf, "this is our side."

"But why? Everyone else is either blue or tangerine?"

"We are not everyone else, we are green!"

"But why grandfather?"

"This is their city, their country, it isn't ours, we are Irish, our land is over the sea, and it is a beautiful island of lakes and rivers, of green fields and mountains, far more beautiful than this wasteland of heather and gorse."

"But why are we here?"

The old man smiled and nodded, "maybe it is your time to know the sad tale of our people. The English drove us out of our homes in our native land, they brought over a new crop and they forced us all to plant it and eat it, then when everyone was eating it, when families were having it for dinner and supper and broke the fast with it in the morning, then they brought in the pest. The pest which ruined all the plants and we starved, the whole island starved, except in the north where their heretic colonizers live. Thousands died and we were forced to go to Dublin and beg any boat that was leaving the island for Britain, there we saw it, all the food, the grain, the lamb being shipped out of the country while thousands starved."

"But why grandfather?" George asked.

"Because we are not like them, and do not divide them they are all jackals who have come out of the same bitch! The English, Scots, Welsh and Cornish, all scum! They use to go to the true church like us, take the same communion as we do, but because one king wanted a divorce and his holy father would not give him one then they drew all the country out of the church, but we stayed faithful George, we stayed true. We will be accepted into heaven as a people, they will all be cast into hell! I am too old to avenge that George, my time has already been and gone, but yours hasn't."

George looked up into his grandfather's eyes, the same twinkling blue of his own, "but I was born here grandfather, I am Scottish."

"No, you were born here George, yes that is right, but you are not Scottish, your blood is Irish and you are your blood, you are Irish. You don't remember the time of hunger, but your blood does George."The old man then sat down, "I came here to Dundee without shoes, the English never even left me those, and I fought to keep your father from starving, but I did it all for you George."

"Me?" George asked.

"Yes you George," the old man replied, "you will be the one who gets revenge for the Dumfries clan. You will get revenge for all the people who died in Ireland, for all the wee bairns I had to bury on the long road to Dublin."

"But how grandfather?" George asked, "I am only ten."

"Study hard George, and when you are old enough head south to London, there in that great sess pit capital of the bastard English go into their parliament, that great palace of satan! There if people say where you are from say that you are from Scotland, that you are a Scot! Then they cannot say that you can't enter, if they say that then they are saying that Scotland is no more theirs."

"But people will know that I am Irish," George replied.

The old man leant back with a broad grin, "today is a new world my child. Today the men in power are not real men, they are not the Caradocs of old, men who rose up from the people and lead them into battle. The new leaders are all leopards with stripes painted over their spots, the Kings of England, all of them are not English, they are Germans, this is the age of the charlatan. Never be afraid to say that you are a Scot and that you are British! But work all the time to bring this kingdom to it's knees!"

Chapter Two:

The two spies, because spies they most certainly were, were barged over the drawbridge and into Caste Hamlet, George leading the way, "you should let me slit them open!" The hag cried above the din.

"No," the blacksmith shouted, "George knows what he's doing, George is always right!"

"It's not good to let someone else do your thinking for you," the hag replied.

The blacksmith stopped, his lower lip budged out as he tried to think of a reply, before he grunted, "shut up you old bitch!" That seemed to cover the situation nicely.

As they reached the drawbridge the two men then broke free and ran over it into the castle, George then turned on his followers and sighed, he had won again, he had imposed his will on them, just as he had on those boys in Dundee all those years ago. "Thank you my friends, you alone have stood by me through the storm."

"Storm?" The hag echoed, "I can't remember no storm."

George ignored her and sighed, "but now isn't the time, we are only one village, we have supporters all over the land, but we are still not strong enough, if we rise up then we will be crushed, it will not even be a contest. It seems like the bully is always stronger, but it won't always be like that. Thank you again, now I must rest," he bowed slightly before striding back into the fortress which was as diminutive as he was.

"What storm?" The hag asked again, "I can't remember no storm."

The sly faced man walked around George's study, noting the catholic paintings and then perusing the books, any one of which could have landed him in the tower. The blond haired man sat brooding, still shaking from what had happened, "they were going to kill us."

Slyface smiled, "but they never, so today is the first day of the rest of your life."

The door opened and George entered, "I am sorry about that gentlemen."

"Well you should be!" Slyface replied, "this is your village, you should keep it in proper order or else we will take it away from you!"

"Maybe I shouldn't have stopped them then!" George snapped. "Maybe the Prince has sent you two to do me in!"

There was an uneasy smile, the blond man was about to reply before Slyface's hand rested on his shoulder, "now come, come George, you know yourself that you aren't worth it."

George's face smarted, but his anger died and he smiled, "yes I guess the Prince has other enemies."

"Besides you are proving useful to us," Slyface replied, "we know that the Ottomans are training up assassins, thousands of them."

Blondie then got to his feet, "what has that got to do with him? Is he with them?"

"No you idiot," Slyface replied, "Mr Dumfries is the one who is giving us their names, every time one of these killers appear here it is our friend here who gives us the information, then they disappear."

"So he is playing both sides?" Blondie replied.

"Not so loud!" George hissed, "do you want to get me killed? I only give you the names because my group is a peaceful one we do not associate with killers."

Slyface grinned broadly, "yes you keep telling yourself that George." Slyface then walked across the room and smoothed his hand over a globe of the world. "Many times the Prince has thought of having you killed, you know and blaming the wolves in the Epping Forest for it."

"There are no wolves in the Epping Forest," George scoffed.

"Oh there are always wolves," Slyface replied, "they come out in carriages from London, but I have always told him, no you are useful to us."

"He wouldn't dare touch me, with soldiers in Servia, Bactria, Mesopotamia and on the Lion Mountain, the last thing he wants is a revolt here, only five leagues from his capital city!"

Slyface looked at him seriously at first and then just shook his head, "you're beginning to believe your own nonsense George, just keep giving us the names and you'll be fine."

"Is he working for us then?" Blondie asked.

George looked at him and shook his head, "where did you find this one?"

Slyface smiled, "well some village must be missing it's idiot."

George nodded, "the crowd has gone now, I trust you can make your own way back to London." They were about to leave when George added, "you know there is one way how you can stop the Ottoman assassins, all of them and it is 100% guaranteed."

Slyface smiled, "well nobody claims to be omnipotent George, tell us."

"The Prince and for that matter the King are friends with the Ottomans, the same Ottomans who are arming and supplying the assassins, why doesn't your prince just tell them to stop it?! These people are not just a bunch of Gloucestershire idiots who cause trouble after too much cider, no they are well armed and they moved through the forests of Africa, the mountains of Bactria or the corridors of the Palace of Westminster all the same."

At that Slyface smiled, "maybe we are all playing a double game George not just you."

Evening fell over Castle Hamlet, and the Thames seemed like the river of Styx between this world and the next, few boats passed along it, mainly smugglers this time of night. George looked at the river again, and he thought of his grandfather, his hatred had kept him going all these years. George looked back over the dark waters into his childhood. He had often stood looking out from his grandfather's window onto the Tay, he had watched the boats there but they were different boats than these, there they were trawlers, and the quayside was always lined with their families, with each boat arriving the people went home, but sometimes there was a boat which never came back and a family which never went home.

Dundee was a bleak place, and it virtually vanished in the winter beneath the snow, only one place seemed to give an escape from this world and that was the church. To enter through it's doors you left the greyness of Scotland behind you and entered a part of Rome. The windows had to be put high up so that people couldn't hit them with their stones. The light was a mix of sunlight and candlelight, and there was always the smell of incense. George felt sorry for the Scots who never had a world like this to enter. On Sundays George would look over the statues as if they were people who had been frozen by time itself.

One Sunday George remembered well, he sat next to his grandfather as the priest began to give his sermon, and then it seemed that the priest's eyes seemed to fix on his grandfather, "we in Christ's church have never been the friend of schismatics, however what the Red Tsar is now doing in Muscovy is a crime against God himself, and he will be judged harshly for it on judgment day. He and his animals will burn in hell for it, I can assure you of that." The priest's voice was unapologetic Irish, the kind of voice which started rebellions, his eyes drilled into George's grandfather's, but the old man never looked away he met the priest's stare and then some."Churches are burning all the way from the borders of Lithuania to beyond the Urals and a new creed is standing in it's stead. A creed which doesn't believe in breakaway bishops and patriarchs that are a false as a six pound note because it is a creed which believes in no God, only believes in the devil!"

George's grandfather straightened his back and threw his shoulders back, it was then the priest who looked away. No one had ever looked at him like that and the priest felt like casting him out of the church altogether but there was something about him, a power which contrasted with his starved and frail frame.

As they went up to take communion the priest paused before giving the wafer to him, "I hope you paid attention to what I said today Shamus."

"Of course I always do Father," he lied.

As they walked out George whispered to him, "what was the priest talking about Grandfather?"

His old eyes fell on him, "bollocks George, bollocks!" He then ushered him out of the church and they were back in the cold of Dundee again, into a world drained of colour. Shamus nodded, what sin had he committed to end up here?

"He said that the Red Tsar was killing a lot of people," George whispered.

The old man nodded, "yes so he is and they deserve it."

"He said that they were killing thousands," George murmured.

The old man nodded, "yes and thousands deserve it."

"How can so many people deserve it?" George asked.

"Look around George, look at Dundee, are you saying that no one deserves to be killed here? Look at the rich people, eating five dinners a day when we are only having one, they deserve it, they could spare some of their smoked salmon for us couldn't they? Look at the English who come up here, why are they here for? It isn't their country, they deserve to be sent back home dead, look at the Protestants with their church which was founded by two men in a smoky backroom one night, because they were short of money, don't they deserve to be killed?"

"Just for going to a different church grandfather?" George asked.

"Of course," he roared, "that's where the Blues and Tangerines go Sunday morning after beating the crap out of each other saturday night. To enter that church is a short cut to hell. Doesn't a vicar, or pastor or whatever they call themselves who is leading people into hell, doesn't he deserve at least a Quarry Bank slapping? That is just Dundee, couldn't we round up five hundred at least to shoot here? Now imagine Muscovy and that is a vast country, starting in Europe and finishing in Asia, imagine if we did the same there, then it would be thousands wouldn't it George?"

"So the Father is wrong?"

"Yes the father is wrong."

"Is that what the Pope says as well?."

"Oh yes the Pope says that as well, only yesterday he was cursing the Muscovite churches to hell, now they are there he is crying about the fact that they are being burnt down and their priests executed."

"So is the Pope wrong?"

The old man nodded, "yes the Pope is wrong as well. Those priests have been feeding their poison to the people for long: 'Obey the King.' 'Let the rich be rich and let your children starve to death, it is Jesus's way.' No it's not Jesus's way, it is their way and they are being dealt with now."

"But the Pope is infallible," George replied.

The old man shrugged, "sometimes he is."

George frowned, "then why do we go to that church if we are not Catholics?"

The old man smiled, "we do not go to that church because we are Catholics, we go to that church because we are Irish! And the English want us to be Protestants, that's why we are Catholics! The Scots, the Welsh and the Cornish have all bowed down to them, but we haven't! We never will either."

It seemed crazy to George even then to go to a church just to annoy somebody but that was the way it was. As they walked home the old man spoke of the Red Tsar, of how he was moving a backwards country into the modern world. He was a dreamer, maybe that is where George had got it from, as they walked through the bleak streets of Dundee, past people scavenging for firewood and others for food he was thinking of the vast eastern steppe. The old man was marching with the Red Tsar, heading into villages and rooting out *kulaks,* and fighting the last of the white guards . Although there couldn't have been any white guards left by now and they were fighting ghosts.

George was still a Catholic, more as his tribe than his religion, but in his heart he didn't really believe in anything. He had started to learn about Allah and the Koran, he had read it, he quoted from it, but he didn't believe in it either. George sat and looked over the river, he never wanted to go back to Dundee, there was nothing there for him now anyway.

Outside the hag washed her clothes in a stream, as it got darker and darker, the blacksmith shook his head, "you are a daft old bat, washing your clothes in there they are dirtier when they come out than when you put them in."

At that moment a garishly looking figure emerged from the tavern with trousers of silver and red stripes and sideburns which cut down into his face like two hedges of ginger wire. He checked his pocket watch before heading over to the blacksmith, "good morrow, I am Enver Mull."

"Good morrow," the black smith nodded.

"Yes good morrow," the hag replied, "I tell you I have always washed my clothes in this stream, as my mother did, and her mother."

"Maybe it was clean back then, but it ain't now. Can you even see what you are doing?"

Mull bowed theatrically, "I am from the Globe Theatre in London."

The black smith looked at him and shrugged, "thanks for telling us."

"I am here to see George Dumfries."

"That's why most people come here," the black smith replied.

"His castle is over there," the hag nodded, "you ain't here to kill him are you?"

"No, I am here to arrange his theatrical debut," Mull announced grandly.

"What's one of them?" The hag grunted.

The blacksmith just rolled his eyes. Mull then pranced across the road as if he was on stage, leaving a whiff of cologne behind him, "thank you Sir, kind lady."

The hag looked around her to see who he was talking to.

Mull then strode like a turkey towards the castle's door, over the pathetically small drawbridge and a moat which had long dried up and now stenched of rubbish, of course Mull couldn't smell it above his own overpowering perfume. He pulled off his white glove before tapping against the door. He then waited, looking back at the black smith and touching his forelock, the black smith just shook his head. The great medieval door drew open and an old Irishman with a red nose looked at him, "I'm sorry Sir, but we do not need a jester, Lord Dumfries doesn't agree with the exploitation of-"

Mull waved him away, " a jester I am not, I am from the Globe Theatre in London, that centre of fine art and culture."

The Irishman wearily nodded, "Lord Dumfries doesn't believe in theatres, they are too borge, borg, -er."

"Bourgeoisie is the word you are searching for my good man and I do have an appointment to see George."

The Irishman wearily sighed, "follow me."

"Have you worked for Lord Dumfries long?" Mull asked.

"Long enough," the Irishman replied.

As Mull was shown into the study Dumfries was still looking out into the darkness, the door opened and the dandy pranced in, "good morrow Enver Mull."

George smiled, "look I don't know what language that is, but whatever it is I don't speak it, only English I am afraid."

Mull smiled, "it is not some strange dialect that I speak, I am Enver Mull from the Globe Theatre."
George smiled, "well of course you are dear."

"I am here to offer you the chance to appear on stage."

George leant back and just looked at him, " you're not serious are you? Who sent you?"

"I am from the Globe Theatre," Mull protested.

George straightened his back, "I am a member of His Britannic Majesty's parliament, not a milk bottle juggler!"

"No, I want you to be in a show where you will have a chance to put over your political message to a thousand people in the heart of the capital, every night of the week save Sunday!"

George drew forwards, "really?"

"Imagine every night a thousand people hearing your message, in a place where the government can't censor."

"Apart from Sunday," George corrected.

"Oh yes," Mull agreed, "apart from Sunday."

George stood back and smiled, how long would Enver Mull had lasted in the streets of Dundee back in those days? George would have gotten a beaten for just talking to him. Then he thought of himself stood on stage exposing his political theories, in fact his theories on everything, the limelight shining on his twinkling blue eyes. That would be the start of the yellow brick road which would lead him to the royal palace where he would turf the King out of his throne and then occupy it himself. Then however he returned back to earth, the gritty, crappy world where dreams don't come true and there's a crock of shit at the end of the rainbow. "There isn't a rat hole in this country where Prince Tony doesn't stick his snout into."

Mull straightened his back, "not in The Globe Theatre he doesn't! Some things in this country are still sacrosanct, the Prince would never send his men into my theatre because he knows that they wouldn't leave alive!"

George drew back and gazed over the blackening mud and out to sea, there was a different world out there, a world that was passing him by, he had to get off this island, Scotland, England, it was all rubbish, it wasn't his island anyway.

"So what do you say my good Sir?" Mull bowed extravagantly.

George smiled, "I never make decisions so quickly, let me think about it."

Further up the Thames there stands the greatest of all senates, the mother of all parliaments, a huge gothic palace which shamed any of the King's. A statue of Cromwell stood in front of it, as two fingers to the king. Two chambers lay inside, the Lords was the larger but had been in decay for years, living skeletons sat there in puddles of their own urine as spiders weaved cobwebs around them, when they died it was weeks before people noticed and removed the bodies. The commons was dingy and cramped in comparison, however it was the nobler place and it was from here that the country and empire were ruled. The common folk sent their representatives here, kilted figures from the Hebrides, Danes from Zetland and warriors from the Foyle fotress. The government of Prince Anthony had won with a landslide, but most people hadn't voted for him, but then that was the way it always was. Tony had come in saying that the mild corruption of his predecessor wouldn't be tolerated under him, the brown envelopes of money, the cash for questions, all that would go, but the place was as rotten as ever. Tony was not there, he was taking orders not from the King but from the leader of the colonists, in his place was his deputy and he was the most rotten thing in the most rotten parliament.

The government was a line of kilts, the northern Celts occupied the lion's share of the seats, elbowing out their English and Taffy rivals, but at their heart was a true Englishman. John Presley's thick Yorkist voice had been heard speaking out for the poor for a decade in opposition, now their man was in government. He was fat, toad of a man whose half closed eyes swiveled out from sagging bags of old skin. He hadn't challenged Tony for leadership, he was quite happy where he was, he was not a greedy man he just wanted his share.

Once the commons had been a lively place but that was a long time ago now, now they were all working for the colonists, they were all getting the silver. The unimpressive bald man got to his feet, he had to go through the motions he supposed. "You Sir have left the English as second class people in their country, the Welsh, the Scots, the Ulster Scots all have their own parliaments, where they make up their own laws, then they come here and make laws for the English as well, what a bloody cheek! You are English yourself, how can you sit there, amongst all those sporran jockeys and screw over your own people?"

Behind him people cheered and clapped, some patted him on the back and then the house fell silent. Presley then rose to his feet and pulled up his trousers, he then looked around the parliament and held out his hand, he then shook his head, he then held out his hand again. Presley then sat down.

The bald man got to his feet sharply, "ah so you have no answer do you?"

Presley got to his feet again and shook his head, he then coughed, "as always you have showed yourself to be a light weight." That was all that said to the bald man's points as the house erupted in laughter, the house was now full of people who cared little about country, democracy or anything. Some one threw a tomato at the bald man, he use to be a soldier and so never flinched, but he did when a tin of paint hit the ground before him.

"Speaker!" The bald man shouted.

"I think the business of today is concluded Mr Duncan John Smith," the speaker brought down his wooden hammer onto the table which separated the two sides.

"John Duncan Smith," the bald man corrected.

"Whatever your bloody name is, you Sassenach bastard!" The speaker spoke with the same Northern Celtic accent and picked up his purse of silver before he left. Presley accepted the plaudits of his comrades: "Well done Johnny."

"I told him the bloody twat," John replied, "he's come down here from Buckinghamshire or wherever and thinks he can ask me questions, who the bloody hell does he think he is?"

"The leader of the opposition," someone shouted from the other side.

"Opposition? What the hell is that? He's just a bloody wazuck, nothing more than that,"Presley grumbled, he then made his way through the crowd, cracking a joke no one heard but everyone still laughed at. He had only just left the chamber when his hand went inside his pocket and he began to squeeze his Cumberland sausage. He couldn't believe how that bald headed idiot had talked about English people being oppressed, he was English and he didn't feel oppressed.

His secretary was waiting in his corridor and Presley's hand left his Cumberland and took her hand, whisking her up, "is everything alright John?" She was a pretty enough piece, blond and young, nice, ripe fruit.

"Oh it's that bald headed bastard, he has given me a headache," he grumbled as they headed down the corridor. "I mean I know he has to say some thing, and he can't actually say anything that is important because the colonists won't like it, but by heck what a load of twaddle he comes out with. I mean how could he ever be prime minister? He's such a twat even his own hair has left him, that's how popular he is, look at my head, I still got as much hair now as when I was twenty!"

"Is anything the matter?" She asked with that wide eyes innocent look of hers.

"Yes there is a problem, a big problem, I've got a stiffey," he moaned. He was in a half panic as he threw open the first office door, there the blind man stood laughing as his dog licked cream off a naked woman. "Sorry," John coughed, "he might not be able to see a foot in front of him but he knows his way around a pair of tits."

They carried on down the corridor and John continued, "all day listening to that crap, bald headed bastard, I've been thinking of doing this." He then pushed open another office door and almost threw her inside, nailing her down on a table before tearing his trousers off, "this is the big problem!"

The secretary looked in feigned awe because in truth the Cumberland hardly emerged from beneath his great gut of fat. Presley tore open her blouse and began to slobber over her breasts like a Saint Bernard. In his younger days he had been a merchant sailor, spending months at sea, with only the five fingered shuffle to entertain him, now he was making up for it.

Outside the corridor was filled with the sound of people rushing from the chambers, suddenly the door flew open. John turned around like an angry wart hog as Robin Crook tumbled in with his secretary. Crook looked as if he had weasel blood in him, resembling the Sherfiff of Nottingham in children's books with his red beard, he was another kilt wearer. Presley roared like a great dog confronted by a smaller rival, "bugger off Crook! Can't you see that I'm shoveling?!"

"There's nowhere else," Crook stammered.

"Then do it in the corner and don't make much noise!" The couple already joined at the hips tumbled into the corner.

John then lashed out with his foot and hammered the door shut, "were you born in a barn?"

So there we have it, the mother of all parliaments, George seldom went there, and when he tried to speak he was only drowned out by the hoard of government stooges. It had been a loftier place under the other party, one of their top men had had a baby with his secretary and he had made a tearful speech. He had said that as a gentleman he would have to resign from the King's government, he could not serve his Majesty as a man without honour. The previous Prime Minister had had a girlfriend but he had kept that a secret until he had left power, these days however there was no need of secrets, because there was no shame. Crook had a wife and Presley had a wife who looked like a pantomime dame, but who cared? Other members roamed around the common land looking for young men to sodomise. The houses of parliament were now as dirty as the river running outside it.

The Lords should have been cocooned from all this but they weren't, a new breed were parting the cobwebs, people whose blood were no more noble than the old hag, but the royalty they had was on their bank notes that they handed over to Prince Tony, with that they became Lords and Sirs. The moral foundations of the parliament were rotting and it was known as far away as Muscovy where the Red Tsar laughed as how that great pinnacle of morality, the British Houses of Parliament, resembled more a Portuguese *casa das putas*.

Chapter Three:

George never slept entirely and long after Enver Mull had left he stood by the window, his eyes brooding. He thought back to a night a long time ago and a long way from here, when he had last escaped this bleak island. He had caught a boat there from Dundee, heading down the coast of Africa until he reached the final land before the ice. It was a place that he had no business in, and he knew that as he headed down the gang plank. He looked out to Table Mountain, no one had asked him to come, no one knew him here, but he had read enough to know there was trouble here and he would stoke it up.

It had taken him a long time to earn the trust of anyone here, months passed with George heading into the poorest areas and running his mouth off like a broken tap about how there should be no rich people or poor, how the world's wealth should be spread evenly like butter on a slice of bread. Of course at first the natives never wanted to believe a white man, but he talked so much, and there was some thing different about his accent and manners, and he was much taken by women of, let us say, a darker persuasion.

Eventually he found a guide and it was a cold, moonless night as they headed through the scrawny bush land, God only knew why any white man would want this place, but then they were people who had left Europe for one reason or another, but everyone is running from something.

 "Where are we going?" George hissed.

 The tall black man glanced back, "you wanted to meet the rebels didn't you? Well we are going to meet them." He then smiled, "are you afraid white man?"

"No," George lied. Africa at night is a land filled with noises, in the shadows there came a bellowing roar, "what's that?"

The black man laughed, "that is only a lion."

"A lion!" George started.

The African laughed, "this is Africa George, you do not need to be afraid of the lions here, it is the people who you need to be afraid of."

"You think they will kill me these people we are about to meet?" George ventured.

The guide shook his head, "maybe but not because of your colour George, we have a lot of whites here with us, they are mainly Jews though. You are not a Jew though are you George?"

"No," he replied. This will no doubt amaze many people who had followed the life of George Dumfries, and read his speeches in Hansard, but back in those days he never spoke much about the struggles between the Canaanites and the Philistines, he was more vexed on the terrible struggle of the black man to achieve equal rights in his own continent, he hardly mentioned Jews and Arabians back then.

"Then what would the problem with me be?" George asked, looking into the shadows, not sure if a lion did attack he would stop him with this musket, what if it never fired? Muskets were as about as reliable as a woman with money.

"Why are you here George?"

"Look I told you that a dozen times, do you not believe me?"

The black man smiled, "tell me again."

"I don't see the world as black people and white people," George replied, "I see the world as oppressed and oppressors. You people here are being oppressed , just like my people the Irish."

"Then why aren't you there?" The black man replied, "helping your own people?"

"There is more chance of victory here than back home," George replied, "that is why I am here to fight for freedom."

"That might be your problem," the black man replied.

"What?" George asked as the world seemed to get darker around them, but no reply came and so he asked something else, "so where are we going?"

"There is someone I want you to meet."

"Who is that?"

"The butcher."

George felt his blood freeze, "the butcher?"

"Yes George, why are you here in Africa?"

George snapped with irritation, "like I already told you, to help you free yourselves from the whites."

The guide smiled, "why?"

"So you could have freedom."

The guide laughed, "you know to the north we have already driven the whites out, they were the Portuguese, do you think that they are free now?"

"Sure."

"Well they are not, the land is too rich there, that riches pays for all it now, that is why Kestrel is sending so many men over from Havana, we need that wealth. Without it we are sunk. That is why his soldiers are in Africa, do you think they want Africa to be free?"

"Yes, of course," George replied.

The tall man shook his head with a smile, "no he doesn't, if they are free they will not give him their wealth, and without that he is sunk."

"Why are you telling me all this?" George replied, not sure if the man wasn't working for the other side.

"Because if you are with us you must know the truth now, I do not want you to believe what Kestrel says about fighting for freedom and then to find this out and betray us."

"I would never betray Kestrel," George replied like a man in love.

"We shall see," the black man replied.

George could smell the blood even before they came to the clearing and was preparing himself for it but when he got there it was worse than he could ever had imagined, his eyes crossed ten headless corpses before they met those of the butcher himself. Like a mantis he rose slowly to his feet, holding the head of his last victim with one hand and the dripping blade with the other. He had the eyes of a devil, most men would look away but George never.

"Who are these people?" George looked towards the corpses.

"They are people who fled the north, we have kept them here until our comrade could come, now he is here and he has judged them and found them all guilty," the guide then gave a cruel smile, "he never finds anyone innocent."

"They are imperialists then?" George asked.

"No," the guide replied, "they are poor people."

"Then they were fighting for the rich, their lackeys?" George tried again.

"No, they were fighting for their country and their people, their crime, why they are being executed is because they want to run their own country not let Kestrel run it for them."

George nodded but ignored what he had said, "does he speak?"

"Not English," the guide replied, "he killed a lot of Portuguese, then when they left there was talk of having an election, a parliament like you have back there in London, of course we couldn't allow that."

"Why?" George gasped, "you would have won anyway."

The guide smiled, "we would have lost anyway, our man would have come in second. You see this is Africa and people vote according to their tribe and our friends have no tribe, they are a rag bag of the love children of the Portuguese and the people who use to clean their houses, they had no tribe, they speak no language other than the language of their masters. So the butcher first drove out the other two parties from the city, butchering as many of them as he could. Then one from our side a man emerged who started talking about dividing the wealth of the country amongst the poor, so of course we had to kill him, we killed him and thousands of his followers, and thousands more who only knew him, or had talked to him, all had to die."

George crossed himself, "oh my God, but what did Kestrel do about it?"

The guide smiled broadly, "it was Kestrel's men who did most of the killing, we couldn't trust the people there to do it, so we did it ourself, got rid of this Robin Hood who didn't like empires."

George drew back, he had believed in Kestrel, believed that he was only in Africa as a liberator, part of him couldn't believe what he was hearing, but in his heart he knew that it was right. He knew that Kestrel was the same as Prince Anthony, a devil masquerading as a man, and yet he ignored it, shoved it to a corner of his soul.

One woman was left alive and she cowered at the butcher's feet, George nodded towards her, "what is he keeping her for, the bed?"

"No Sir," the guide replied.

George's eyes then met his, "then what then?"

"This one is yours," he then looked down at the blade of a knife handed towards him.

George recoiled, "you can't be serious."

"What better way to show that we can trust you George?" The guide's face opened with a broad smile.

George then looked towards the woman, she was a pretty girl, with a delicate face, she whimpered too weak to fight or to scream. George looked down at the blade again.

"So are you with us George?" The guide mocked.

George hovered, the two black men looked at him, George knew that if he didn't do it he would be next, he gritted his teeth and then snatched up the blade, before he strode over to the woman. "you imperialist bitch!"

The guide laughed as George hurled his blade into the defenseless woman, "there George congratulations, you're part of the revolution now!"

George remembered that woman, usually late at night, but she had deserved it, he told himself that, if Kestrel had marked her she was guilty, he had done the world a favour. It was almost as if there was something inside his head, something that limited him reaching the logical conclusion. He couldn't accept that Kestrel was wrong, like the old priest back in Dundee, who read the bible, who prayed but never reached the final logical conclusion at the end of it all. Morning rose and he hadn't moved from the window and had not slept. He would go to the globe, he had had enough of this place, he had to get away.

An uneasy silence settled over the village as Enver Mull's carriage pulled up in front of the castle. The dandy got out and looked around the village, what a ghastly place, how could anyone live here? He had a fantasy of driving the whole place into the river and building some town houses here, after all it was not far from London. George came out , in a big floppy hat which looked like he'd stolen it from a lady man rather than a musketeer. There was only the hag and a fisherman there to see him go and he gave them a raised fist salute.

"Give them hell George," the fisherman shouted.

George nodded and they both waved as the carriage pulled away, the fisherman's head than sank, "he's a fool isn't he?"

The hag laughed, "so you've noticed have you?"

Enver Mull lowered the handkerchief from his mouth as they left Castle Hamlet behind them. George smiled, "you don't care much for those type of places do you Mr Mull."

Mull shook his head, "I've been to better places."

George smiled, "I haven't, those places give the world it's Alexanders, Cromwells and Watt Tylers."

"And is that a good thing?" Mull replied.

George never replied, his face just wisped with a smile.

The Globe Theatre was London's palace of fools, or rather London's other palace of fools. The theatre was a bawdy affair standing over the Thames, where the lower strata of society came to laugh at the upper level's misfits, both on the stage and in the audience. There were gays dressed as women, crow faced women who had never found husbands and pompous figures who had always been too grand to work. It's candle lights formed a clearing of yellow on the dark river which stretched over to the other side, throwing back the rowing boats of the patrons heading over to see the awful plays. The 'entertainment' often went late into the night, for husbands who had been thrown out by their wives and they were always the same old dire pieces: 'The ill fated lovers', "the Prince of Denmark' , and 'the King of Scotland', even the insomniac was asleep by the last one and it was usually met by a chorus of snores, descending from the top balcony to the pit. These plays had been performed since the time of Good Queen Bess, and people spoke of their quality but in truth their best talent lay in sending folk to sleep. The government's big wigs would often come down to see the Scottish play and laugh at the accents, how Middle Saxons thought Scots spoke.

As the carriage arrived George looked over the theatre and then breathed in the air, as dirty as London ever is but it smelt sweet today as he stepped down, yes this was where he belonged. If only he could marry both the worlds, the one of power and the one of adoration. He looked over the building as if it was magical castle inhabited by fairies. Mull then stepped out, "really we don't have much time, I mean a new show needs a lot of rehearsal."

George held up his hand to silence him, 'don't worry Dearie," George winked, "we'll have time for it all."

Already his manner was agitating Mull, but he had to put up with it because he was their star, he was the man everyone was going to turn up to see. He was one for the chattering classes, they had always thought George was a fool and this would be the final proof, the final unmasking of the would be Simon Bolivar to find more a David Icke.

George entered the theatre without invitation and stepped up onto the stage before gazing around him in admiration, yes this is where he belonged, he then turned round to Mull, "alright let's get started."

Enver nodded, "I'll just fetch the script."

"You're George Dumfries aren't you?"

George looked over to a stage hand painting a design in the wings, and he saw the glazed eyes of a follower, "yes I am."

"It's great work you are doing."

"Thank you, just trying to put our democracy back on track," George even bowed slightly.

"What you say about the wars that the Prince wages, I mean someone needs to say it," the stage hand replied.

"Thank you."

"So what are you doing here?"

"Oh I thought I might take part in one of Mr Mull's productions."

"Why?"

George smiled, "oh you know, get the message over to more people."

The stage hand stood back, "what here? In the Globe Theatre?! With Enver Mull?"

George nodded.

The stage hand shook his head, "you are wasting your time here Mr Dumfries, this place isn't about that."

George smiled, "oh I think I can handle Enver Mull."

"You won't Mr Dumfries," the stage hand warned.

George smiled, "we shall see."

News of a new play had travelled fast and there were more boats than usual heading over the Thames from what use to be West Saxony. Many wanted to see the star Manuel Broadmoor, he was a tall, stick insect of a man who told few jokes but pulled faces and shouted and was thought hilarious by the lower ranks of London. Broadmoor was making his comeback after escaping (some said) from an asylum. George sat in the wings that first night and watched as the comic headed out onto stage to some cheers, he bowed with that old smile of his. Then a boo came, Broadmoor glanced towards it and his face began to crack. "He's lost it," George whispered to the stage hand, "they never come out of those nut houses the same as they go in!' Broadmoor then curled up like a hedgehog and looked as if he was about to burst into tears.

Someone heckled, "come on you bastard! We're here to laugh not cry!"

George smiled and then looked at the stage hand, "you see."

George's smile slowly fell though as Broadmoor slowly unfurled himself and as the crowd saw again his big grin they erupted, "I am the King of France!" The crowd booed then laughed as Broadmoor then paraded himself along the stage making obscene gestures, and the whole theatre thundered with applause. Sometimes it was the King of France sometimes it was the King of Spain, depending who was irritating the English the most at the time, it was never the

King of Scotland though, that would have landed Broadmoor straight in the tower of London.

George had to kill his own smerk, "it's not real comedy though is it? I mean where are the jokes, how can you repeat that to your friends in the tavern?"

"But he's got something though," the stage hand replied.

'Bastard!' George thought, 'this wanker is going to upstage me!' George smiled, "oh yes he's got something," he admitted aloud, "I just hope that it's not catching."

He then felt a hand on his shoulder, he turned, it was Slyface, "you're taking this a little too seriously aren't you?"

George felt a chill run through him, of course he knew that the Prince would be able to send men even here, he would have been stupid to believe Mull, "I take everything seriously!"

Slyface then nodded and smiling drifted out to the audience again, not only were the spies here but they had free run of the place!

Broadmoor then strutted along the stage in a half dance, "I'm out now! They let me out! They let me out!"

The laughter was deafening, easily drowning out the grinding of George's teeth.

Wisely Mull let all the commotion die down before he played his next trump card. The crowd was beginning to nod off as a Polish princess edged out onto stage, she had once been a beauty and even now she was charming. The crowd always loved to see an aristocrat who had fallen on hard times, and they went mad when Mull had announced that she was a princess, it didn't matter if she was Polish or Portuguese, she was one of them! The first rotten tomato was thrown of the night and Mull took that as his cue to leap on stage and announce:

"And now my Lords, Ladies and gentlemen, fresh from His majesty's house of commons, the Right 'onourable Sir, Lord George Dumfires!"

The house fell silent no-one knew he had been coming here, a member of the government! Maybe he was here to shut the place down and have them all arrested! A silhouette stepped out onto the stage, it was so silent you could hear the mice chew at the curtains, then the light shone onto him. Then all saw, George Dumfries, the member of parliament for Castle Hamlet, dressed as a tiger! The globe didn't know what to make out of it, then he started to sing, a truly dismal song about how nice it was to be a cat!

"It's George Dumfries!" A Whig gentleman stammered, looking up from his prostitute's left breast.

"He'll be thrown out of the commons for this!" A Tory added waking from the right breast.

The Princess pulled at his whiskers and then joined in the song about how much she loved her cat. But no one could hear it, the crowd was thundering and Enver Mull beamed with contentment. This year the Globe had outdone itself, to have a member of parliament here showing himself to be a fool! Confirming what they all knew already. Who would be here next year, the Prince himself no doubt?

Slyface smiled from the audience as well, "I think George must be cleverer than we gave him credit for or he can read the Prince's mind."

"Why?He looks like a prat to me," Blondie replied.

"No, on the contrary he is very clever. The prince has been worrying for a long time about how popular George has been getting, even intelligent people have started to listen to him. I have been waiting for the order to come any day now to kill him, but now I don't think it will ever come, he has bought himself some time at least."

Chapter Four:

George watched from the wings as Slyface drank from a huge frothy tankard, by midnight he would be too drunk to watch anything. George reached for his coat and pulled it on quickly.

"Where are you going?" The stage hand asked.

"Out."

"Maybe Enver will want you for the finale."

George smiled, "then he will be disappointed, I've done my bit now I am out of here." George headed out into the cold night, there were no carriages, they were waiting until the end of the show, no one would leave this riot early! He would have to walk across town. He didn't mind walking, normally when a carriage driver saw it was him they would start on some political discussion with him, which would start off civil enough and then became heated, even more so when they found out that they weren't getting a tip. "Mr Mull will be disappointed will he?" George chuckled to himself, "oh that breaks my heart."

Night crept over the gothic battlements of the palace of Westminster, the smoke of the night's fires still cloaking it's tower. A pair of knickers hung from one of the windows, there were sounds of singing from another, as George walked towards the parliament a tankard flew out of one of the windows and bawdy argument started, every word of which could be heard in the street below:

"Our deal was to share power, you would be in charge first, then you would step aside for me," a Scottish voice growled.

"There was no such agreement," a crisper, slightly effeminate replied.

"You're a liar!" The Scottish voice roared.

A silence followed, "well of course I am. You don't seem to mind when I go downstairs and lie to the country but you don't like me lying to you."

George walked forwards and smiled at the sentries stood by the gates, "are they having another tiff?"

The sentries laughed, "yes it's every night now, I do not know how this government stays together."

"The devil looks after his own officer," George replied.

"Do you want to go in there?" The other sentry asked.

"Yes I have a meeting with Lord Pantsdown," George replied.

"At this hour?"

"Now come on, you know that this is the best time to catch him awake," George smiled.

The sentry laughed, "go on then Sir."

 Pantsdown's office was high up in the palace, the ravens quarreled outside his window for the scraps of meat he tossed out. Pantsdown smiled as he threw it, it was human meat, he was getting rid of a political victim, slowly, very slowly. From here he could watch the goings on in this asylum, he could see the honourable members , he could see them fornicate often, if that's what you called it. He had had his time, he had had sex with his secretary as well, it was almost a right of passage now. Everyone knew this but no one said anything when he sat in pompous judgment of others. There was a fat man who when he talked to the young ladies of the party liked to touch their legs. When he had heard of this Pantsdown had come down on him like a Lutheran minister talking about the last days. No one in the whole country ever called Pantsdown a hypocrite, no paper, no opponent and not even the fat man himself, that was Pantsdown's power.

Slowly George climbed up the steps, the lanterns burnt dim this high up and the rats crossed his path unchallenged. A new breed of rat had come into the country recently, people said that they had arrived with the Hanoverian kings and they were bigger and more brutal than their black cousins, and had quickly killed the lot of them. George was climbing these steps because he was inpatient, he made great speeches and people believed what he said but it didn't move them to take to the streets and do something about it. There had to be another path to power. In his heart he did have some kind of respect for this place, what it was meant to stand for, but his grandfather's old hatred burnt in him and he imagined blowing the whole place up.

Pantsdown thought back to the day that he had come to England, his accent thick with Belfast, but he had gotten rid of that and now he spoke like he had been born in a manor house. He had joined the navy and had sailed far to the east and gone into battle in the jungles, facing death, all those risks he had been through had been for him to have this life, for him to spend his last days here in an office over looking the palace of Westminster. If he had died then he would have lost the gamble, but he hadn't and he had won, and he seemed to have a smug faintly amused smile permanently fixed on his face.

A knock came at the door and Pantsdown beckoned George in like a sixth former called into the headmaster's study, "enter." The door opened and he got slightly to his feet, "George old chap, how the devil are you?"

"Fine, I just thought that I would come over."

"Sorry I missed your show, how did it go?" Pantsdown smiled.

"You know about that?" George gasped.

Pantsdown leant back in his armchair, "I know about everything. I am thinking of entering the world of entertainment, maybe as a narrator in plays and the like."

"Yes why not, it is always good to do something artistic," George replied.

"Oh it's nothing to do with that," Pantsdown replied, "I would expect to be paid and well paid for it, I'm sure that my friends will arrange me some work, you know just to keep the larder stocked with sherry.Now why are you here at this most Godly hour?"

"Look I thought that maybe we should work together."

"Oh you've not come over to talk politics have you," Pantsdown moaned, "or do you want me to go on stage with you, no doubt with my face blacked up singing about my dear old mater in the cotton fields? It's been so long since you have come here and now you are talking that old stuff."

"Politics is our bread and butter Sir," George replied.

Pantsdown shook his head, "maybe," he smiled, "well maybe we could have a bit of politics, would make a change. How can I help you?"

"Look we need to work together, my party and your party," George took a seat without being invited to and leant forwards.

"My party is a little larger than yours," Pantsdown condescended.

"Yes, it is."

"I mean your party only has one man in parliament, you."

"But still I have a following, mine is a grass roots movement which is seizing the imagination of people in the big cities," George enthused.

Pantsdown gave a strained smile, "what a great loss to the world of advertising you are George."

George ignored him, "together it might prove enough to take control of the country," George urged.

Pantsdown nodded, he didn't say anything, he bit his lip as if he was contemplating what he said but he was doing it not to laugh.

"Look we have to stop these wars, all these wars that the government keeps getting us into!" George urged.

Pantsdown nodded, "yes of course." He shook his head, amazed at George's stupidity, or was this some kind of test, had the colonists sent him?

"I would serve under you," George urged.

Pantsdown bore a fruity smile and his eyebrows rose.

"Well not in that way, you know what I mean though." George expected him say something but Pantsdown said nothing so he tried again, "we have to stop the Prince, we don't know what he will do next."

Pantsdown nodded, and then looked around, "look George I don't know what game this is."

"We need to get rid of this crazy man," George urged.

Pantsdown then coughed loudly.

"Are you alright Sir?" George leant forwards,.

"Yes I am alright George, I just wanted you to shut up. The Prince isn't our problem, he doesn't start the wars, he just follows the colonists into any war they declare."

"And that is his problem! That is why he must leave power!" George snapped.

"And if it wasn't him who would it be? He is nothing, he is just following orders."

"Exactly, it shouldn't be like that! The British prime minister shouldn't be taking orders off any foreigners!" George replied.

"But he does and so do most people around here," Pantsdown smiled.

"What about you then?"

Pantsdown smiled, "me? You don't know anything about me George. But I know about you, I know that you are working for the colonists."

"That's a lie!" George snapped.

"We all are," Pantsdown smiled.

Only now did George see Pantsdown for the sinister man he really was, he seemed to own the shadows he sat in. "You can't be," George protested, "the Whigs protested when Prince Anthony invaded Mesopotamia."

Pantsdown got to his feet and turned around and walked over to the ravens, "I do not know why you came here tonight George, I hope you don't believe what you say. I suggest you get back to your cabaret to make the curtain call."

George paused, there had to be something else to say, but there wasn't, he left and cursed. He almost passed Slyface on the stairs, the spy only emerged from an alcove as George ran down. The agent then headed to Pantsdown's room the door was still open, the Lord's eyes rested on him as he went to close it.

"Good evening officer," Pantsdown nodded.

"What did he want?"

"Who George? It's hard to say, I don't know if he was serious or not, he looked serious," Pantsdown replied, returning to the ravens.

Slyface entered, closing the door, "I guess he is an actor now."

"Yes that might be it, he is no idiot," Pantsdown replied, "I mean the idiots out there swallow what I say, but he shouldn't, he must remember what I did."

"What do you mean?"

Pantsdown smiled, "the Whig party was an inoffensive group of idiots before I entered it, I turned it into a party of war, does he not know that? I pushed for war against Servia, I lied to the core of my being, I said that the province of Methodia was 95% Ilyrian and only 5% Serv, I told that lie over and over again."

"How was it a lie?" Slyface asked.

Pantsdown looked at his face, trying to read it and then he drew the shadows more around him. "It was not just a lie but impossible, in that province there are more than two races there are also Gypsies and Turks, what percentage do they fall into? There are also Ottoman Slavs, maybe you could say they were Servs, but

I wouldn't call them that and neither would they. I kept saying it back in those days and I waited for someone to say that, I even had an reply prepared, but no one ever questioned it, no one ever questions me anymore, it has become boring."

Slyface drew forwards, "why?"

"Everyone knows who I am Sir," Pantsdown smiled, "and who I work for. I had to lie because the Prince didn't want a war, so I had to shout and cajole him into it," Pantsdown leant back. "George should know that, he should remember, unless he is losing it."

"You are not even leader anymore of the Whigs," Slyface replied.

"No, no I am not," Pantsdown admitted, the smugness faded from his face for a moment. "And a lot of the work that I did I have seen undone of late. I don't think our friends across the Atlantic see the Whigs as important, so they are prepared to let it slip out of their grasp. They ignore all the good work that I did for them, they are being very foolish."

Slyface only half understood him, "what can we do then?"

"My successor as leader of the Whigs has to fall," Pantsdown pondered.

"What Kennersley? But he is very popular!" Slyface replied.

Pantsdown looked up at him and smiled, "yes isn't he just? But he is also a Scotsman and like all Scotsman he appreciates a wee dram."

"What do you mean by that?" Slyface replied.

"You're not Scottish are you?" Pantsdown asked.

"No Sir."

"Then I shall translate, Edward Kennersley is a drunkard." Pantsdown waited for that information to sink in before he added, "well he isn't, he just likes to be merry once a week, but who doesn't? What I want you to do is to take that information and paint him as someone who is always intoxicated, play on the ethnic images that we have our northern cousins."

"What the Scots?" Slyface's face blanched, "we can't say anything about them, not now."

Pantsdown motioned him to calm down, "don't worry my friend, the Scots will let this one go by, nothing will happen, tell your superiors this. I will talk to people in the party, see if we can't organize a little bit of discontent." Pantsdown's eyes iced with evil.

"But why? Can't we buy him?"

Pantsdown shook his head, "no he is a man who believes in silly things, like fair play and free speech. He is not one of us Sir, we will have another leader, one who will do what he is told, one who speak ill of Muscovy and the Damascans, read the text that we give him, one who will do whatever the colonists want."

"Who is he?"

"He calls himself Nick Compo, he is not a Whig but a Tory who changed parties some years ago, when we saw this problem might occur. He is not a English either, he has only one English grand parent, he is Dutch and he speaks it fluently, his wife is a Catalan, or Italian or some nonsense like that."

"How can we trust such a man?" Slyface protested.

"How can we not trust such a man?" Pantsdown replied. "He will serve us completely, he is not patriotic because he has no country. The future belongs to such men, not to us, we are like the Falklands wolf, our days of running around the windswept islands are coming to an end. "

Pantsdown then looked down onto the palace, he had let Slyface in enough and now he would close the window, "close the door on your way out officer, if you would be so kind."

George walked out through the palace, he would get nothing from the Whigs, he might as well head back to the Globe maybe he would get to make the curtain call at that. He walked past the Abbey, it was strange the House of God was right next to the house of the devil. He followed along the river and looked at the little boats bringing in more and more people, George smiled, a lot of them would be supporters of the Prince, others would follow him, none of them would be Whigs or Tories, it was the way the Prince stole elections, he made a lot of the people who got off those boats British and let them vote in the elections. If anyone else in the world did it Prince Anthony's mouth would open but no one said anything when he did it.

When he got to the theatre he saw the billboard and stopped and cursed, as he saw that it said 'MANUEL BROADMOOR in.' George stopped, and shook his head, "bastard! How can I be second fiddle to that, to that..freak!" George shook his head, what would it take for him to be the lead? In parliament he was a back bencher and here he was the warm up man for a, for a freak! George pushed his way into the theatre and instantly his eyes met those of the Polish princess:

"George thank God you are here, Enver has been asking for you."

The brilliant anger subsided in his eyes and he smiled, "everyone is always asking for me sweetheart." He winked and she felt twenty years younger. "I think that we know the same people."

"Really?"

George then rolled out a long list of names, he rolled his r's in that special Scottish blarney of his, it made Princess Rula feel like the woman she had been when she had crossed the Atlantic and wowed the men there. George was small and certainly the runt of the litter but when his blue eyes twinkled it seemed to melt a woman's heart. Her eyes though went from him in a second as Broadmoor left the stage, "Manuel you were great out there."

The mask though fell and depression swept over the clown again, "they seemed to prefer your act."

George then glided over with that false smile of his, "no Manuel I am just a politician, that will wear off, no you owned that stage out there. This show is about one thing, and one thing only and that is about getting you back to where you belong, the King of show business." With that everyone around them burst into applause. George then drew back as a crowd surrounded Broadmoor, and his eyes flashed with hatred again as he cursed him to hell.

There was little Enver Mull could have done on the second night to top the first night , but he somehow managed it, after George had sang his song about being a cat, he found the audience rise to their feet and applaud. He bowed, thinking that it was for him until he turned to see a frail figure edge out onto stage with flowing grey locks. Then George joined in the applause and even sank to his knees before him, allowing the elderly man to settle his hand on his shoulder.

"Get up George," the old man smiled, "you're embarrassing me."

George then backed away into the wings, "who is that dude?" The tall black man who Mull had brought over from America asked.

"That is Jimmy Vile," George replied, "one of the few, one of the very few ever to be decorated by His Majesty the King and His Holiness the Pope."

The American was unimpressed, so George tried again, "do you know how old that man is?"

The American shook his head, "no."

"102! 102!" George replied.

"So what? Who gives a shit?" The American replied. "The guy is old."

"He is a great man," George enthused, "he has spent his whole life working for charity!"

The American shrugged, "he looks like a broken down old bum to me."

George then drew back and shook his head, "you Americans just don't get it do you? This man is like a Saint, I would die for this man!"

The American shrugged, "still looks like a bum to me."

Chapter Five:

As the week continued relations between the two stars became more fraught, in any theatre there is only one space at the top. George was irritating even in small doses walking around the theatre giving everyone his views on life, the universe and basketball. That was what the tall black man had made his name doing in the colonies, but of course no one had ever heard of him here. The two were an odd couple, Rod towering over George making him look like a dwarf. Even George's mouth shut though when Vile spoke, he would sit in an armchair and expose his views, dropping in one big name after another. Rod just looked at him and shook his head, "how does that dude do a lot for charity, look at all the gold around his wrists?"

George looked at him and shook his head, "you just don't get it do you?"

The cast's show were an odd assortment, one was a strange gangly figure who looked half way between a man and a woman. Vile's eyes settled on him, that was the magic of Vile, he would talk to anyone, one day he would be talking to kings the next day he would be talking to misfits, "you know when I heard your voice the hairs on the back of my neck rose."

"Why was that?" The ladyman replied.

"You know what I thought, I remembered that group of minstrels who I use to know, "he then came out with the names of the most famous people ever to come out of Liverpool and then looked over their faces.

"You knew them?" The ladyman gasped.

He nodded slowly, knowing that he had got yet another one, the world was full of suckers, few people ever saw through him. "Yes I use to do shows with them, they would take my carriage with them over the Pennines. I talked to them a lot," and so it went on, there were two versions of history, the real version and Vile's. The minstrels had taken journeys with him, they had listened to his long monologues, each night they had stopped at his house, but Vile never invited them in. They had thought he was strange then, many people had thought that he was strange but no one had ever said anything.

Broadmoor listened as well, but he was on edge, he had heard what they were saying in London, George's cat dance was the talk of the town. This show was meant to be about him, but he was being eclipsed. George and Vile's voices grated on him, Vile's eyes settled on him, he could read people's faces, he knew that he was losing him: "You know this man is really one of best performers, I remember seeing his comedy shows, he was hilarious."

Broadmoor smiled, that uncertain smile of his.

Vile leant back, "he had a thing when he would throw people out of the theatre, you would go outside the theatre and see them wandering around like lost sheep, it was a riot!" Vile then laughed that false laugh of his which came from the throat not the stomach.

Broadmoor nodded, but he was never sure if he was being mocked. George then drew forwards and blew cigar smoke over the whole proceedings, and said something banal, as always.

"It was hilarious," Vile added and gave that false laugh of his again. The princess then came up and rested her head on his shoulder, George grinned and sucked in on his cigar again. Women liked him and he liked women, that was another thing Broadmoor hated about him.

Then one day an argument flared up when George returned to his dressing room to find his bottle of Cuban rum empty and there could only be one suspect! He headed straight over to Broadmoor's dressing room, but voices were already raised as the big American was there before him, "you took my tobacco man."

Broadmoor drew back, "me, what makes you consider that I am guilty of such a thing?"

Rod just repeated, "you took my tobacco man."

George then stepped forwards, "yes and he took my rum!"

Voices were raised which were heard on stage as the Princess tried to sing 'my village on the banks of the Neiman."

The black man's voice was superseded by George's eloquent tones.

Broadmoor stepped back, "this wasn't your argument George what are you doing here?"

"He is not a man of many words, I am!" George declared.

"You're just a frustrated performer yourself George!"

George nodded and then looked at the others, he tried to think of something clever to say but he couldn't find the words, and so just showed everyone the empty bottle like a prosecutor showing a court evidence. Then he offered it to the comic, "come on you bastard, drink yourself to death!"

"You don't know the demons I have to fight!" Broadmoor protested.

George laughed, "demons or spirits?" The kind brother of Monday was now the evil bastard of Friday. "poor me, poor me, pour me another!"

"Oh that's low," Chester, one of the lesser stars spat.

Broadmoor looked as if he was about to crack, but just headed back to his dressing room and slammed the door. George nodded, he hadn't got him yet, but he would get him. His eyes then met those of the stage hand, and for a moment he saw himself the way the rest of the world did, he was no rebel leader, he was a joke, he had let at least one man down.

George's next humiliation was to come the next day as he and the ladyman were dressed as mannequins and had to do mime together. Although most of London agreed that this was not as funny as the cat dance, to see a member of parliament dance with a ladyman was most amusing. The costumes clung tight enough to their bodies for the audience to see that George's wedding tackle was considerable smaller than the ladyman's. The posher elements followed their peckers with their opera glasses. The two men moved as if through treacle as the musicians played as delicately as they could, the violin only screeching once or twice, and they finished with a bow and the music was drowned out by hoots of laughter. George had made a greater idiot of himself after by saying that his dance partner was not just a ladyman but a great thinker, like Samuel Johnson, but it would have been hard to think of Dr Johnson doing that.

George went back to his dressing room after that dance and threw his head into his hands, what the hell was he doing? A floorboard creaked behind him, he turned round to see a hooded figure, whose face was lost in shadow, "how did you get in?"

"No door is closed to me," the shadow replied.

"Why are you here?"

The hooded figure did not answer just tossed down a pouch, George didn't need to ask what was inside because he already knew. "Kestrel told me to tell you that you are doing well, he reads your speeches in Havana."

George's face lit up, "really?"

"Yes," the hooded man nodded, "but he will not be too sure about all this."

George picked up the bag and looked inside, "these coins are silver."

"The money has dried up, we are no longer getting money from Kabinda, that was the spring of money which paid for it all, now our brother Zedu has turned his back on us."

"Ungrateful bastard!" George snorted, "you were the ones who put him in power."

"Everyone is in the pay of the colonists these days," the hooded figure replied.

"Well I'm not," George replied, but it was met only with silence.

The hooded figure eventually spoke again: "There will be a boat moored off the Isle of Sheppey, near Sherness on Saturday."

"What of it?"George turned around to see the shadow had gone. He got to his feet, there was only one door, he would have seen if he had gone out through it, maybe he had imagined it, but the pouch was still there. He looked at the coins, silver he mused; things must be getting bad for Kestrel. He then began to run things through his mind, he'd pay one of these cockney boatmen to take him down the river. Maybe it was a trap, but then what could they accuse him of going out to see a ship, was that a crime now? Then maybe the trap wasn't from Prince Tony, he remembered the old priest talking about the devil and how the red tsar was his servant, maybe he was right, and Kestrel was not a man to be seen in church either. He looked at the coins as if they were cursed before he leant over and put them back into the purse. For a moment he had an image of Judas hanging from a tree before he put the purse into his pocket. Outside he could hear Broadmoor throw another tantrum, he laughed to himself, "certainly I am not cut out for show business."

Saturday came round quickly enough and as George went out to sing the cat song again, his eyes climbed to the balconies where Slyface had sat all week. As he drank the blond man was talking to a young woman he was hoping to get VD off. Slyface looked drunk, but then he had the night that he had gone to see Pantsdown. After his song he headed back stage where Rod and Broadmoor were arguing again, "look you gonna have to stop stealing my smokes man."

"I have not done anything of the kind!" Broadmoor protested.

George had no hunger for a fight today and avoided them, heading through the back of the theatre pushing open the door that lead down to the river, before Slyface's blond pal stepped out in front of him, "going somewhere George?"

"Yes to the river."

"Oh really why?"

George shrugged, "I'm going to defecate."

Blondie frowned, "you what?"

"I am going to make a little you," George smiled.

"Really?" The blond haired's musket protruded from his cape like a python.

"Yes haven't people been doing that since in Old Father Thames since the Romans built London?"

"You're not going anywhere," Blondie replied.

George cursed until a deep resonant voice came from behind him, "any trouble George?" Rod stepped forwards, tall and black, his ears glistening with gold, his muscular body adorned with tattoos.

George turned and nodded towards the blond man, "this wee lassie is in my way."

Rod stepped forwards.

"I got a gun," Blondie gulped.

Rod snatched the gun with lightening speed and threw it behind him, halfway across the Thames, "no you ain't."

"I am working for the King," Blondie stammered.

Rod grabbed and lifted him off his feet, his eyes drilling deep into his before he hurled him behind him into the river, "I ain't got a King."

"I hope he can swim," George laughed.

"I hope he can't," Rod replied. They watched as he fought the current, that main of blond emerging and submerging as he was carried downstream. "We ain't going to see if he makes it or not,"Rod cursed as the agent vanished into the shadows.

"Keep swimming you bastard!"George shouted, "all the way to France, because when the Prince finds out you let me out of your sight he'll string you up by your balls."

"Does he do that?" Rod asked.

"Lord knows," George growled, "but it strikes me as the kind of thing that would turn that swine on."

George's eyes then settled on the rowing boat and he pulled down a lantern and made circling motions to it. The boat then headed over to him, and George turned towards the black giant, "do you fancy a little boat ride?"

"I've still got some dumb ass song to do," Rod moaned.

"Let Broadmoor sing it, he'll be your friend for life, he is trying to make himself famous again," George laughed, "but he's all washed up, a drunkard."

Rod shrugged, "you know nobody would laugh at that shit back in America, but I don't know the folks out there seem to like him well enough."

George waved them away, "ah they feel sorry for him, after all he's been through. Well I should thank you Sir."

"Don't sweat it," Rod replied, "he had a musket I just evened up the odds. So where are you going?"

"The Isle of Sheppey."

Rod shrugged, "never heard of it."

"There's not much there, and not much has happened there since the Vikings landed there nine centuries ago, but you can come if you want."

Rod looked back towards the theatre, "hell I can't sing anyway and that crap ain't going to make me more famous."

George shook his head, Rod really had a delusion that he was a big star here, he offered out his hand which Rod clamped his considerably larger, ebony hand over.

"You're a good man to have on my side," George smiled.

They watched the boat near, while George looked back to the theatre, he could hear the howls of laughter at Broadmoor's crude comedy and he shook his head, "bastard." He expected Slyface to edge out into the night, but he needn't have worried, he was already asleep on a cushion of his own vomit. The oarsman threw out the rope and George caught it before pulling the boat closer.

"Who's he?" The oarsman pointed to Rod, "you didn't say that you would be bringing any protection."

"My only protection use to be Jesus and the rosary beads, but now I like something a bit more tangible as well," George smiled.

"I ain't never been called that before," Rod smiled.

The oarsman looked across him as he stepped into the moonlight, never had seen such a tall man, he figured black people had to be that big to fight of all the big animals there are in Africa. As he climbed into the boat he watched it sink in the water, he then struggled with the oars, before Rod took them off him and he rowed them out into the river, then the current helped take them down to where the river became more a sea. Rod's oar cut against the waves as George gazed out over the water, feeling free to be off that prison island once more. The mariner looked with wonderment how Rod just rowed, never moaned and wondered if it was because he had been a slave or was because this was like nothing for him "It is the coming back which will be against us," he murmured.

George's eyes settled, "you can row then."

"So where are we going?" Rod asked.

"To see a man."

"What I'm doing all this rowing just to see a dude?" Rod moaned.

"This is no normal man, this is man is like a Jesus for our time, a man who is speaking out for the weak and the poor," George smiled."He is a man who risks his life day and night in the cause of freedom, a man whose heart beats for liberty, who cannot rest whilst there are people being oppressed."

"He must never sleep then," Rod muttered under his breath.

George looked to where he guessed the horizon was and gave himself a contented smile, he had found out about the boat moored off Sheerness and he knew who was on board.

An hour passed before from the southern coast they saw a bridge rise up towards the clouds in a great arch, Rod had never seen anything like it, "what the hell is that?"

"The bridge over the Swale," the oarsman replied, "that is the name of the water which separates the Isle of Sheppey from the Isle of Britain. The lights you see must be Sheerness."

"That's one weird ass bridge," Rod mused looking at the great arch over the narrow waterway that a normal bridge could have easily crossed.

"And that must be the Liberdador," George's face flashed with excitement, rising to his feet to extend his arm towards a large shadow, moored just outside the reach of the twinkling lights of the Sheerness "the pride of the Veneaguan navy!"

"Probably the only one as well," Rod grunted. "Where the hell is Veneagua anyway?"

"South America," George replied, his eyes sparkling as if that made it magical.

"Looks like the ship I escaped from," Rod replied, "only mine had the Yankee flag on it."

"You were a slave?" The oarsman asked in a whisper.

Rod nodded, "I was born free in Africa, but the chains were put on me when I was a child, but it was too late I had already tasted freedom. Those chains never stayed on me for long, that why I am not afraid, many blacks would be, many would be terrified about being sold again, but I know no slave master can cage me."

George watched Rod's muscles flex as he rowed and he knew that this was no idle threat. From the shadows his eyes caught the Veneaguan flag, "ah there it is the flag that is beginning to rival that of *La Isla Grande* as the flag of freedom."

George then called out, *"hola camaradas!"* He shouted again as they got nearer, but still there was only silence.

"This looks like one of them ghosts ships," the oarsman grunted, "they drift across the ocean crewed only by the dead."

"Yes," Rod agreed, "it's probably full of plague rats or some shit like that."

Even George crossed himself, the ship seemed to resemble some lost Cornish castle in the middle of the sea, "maybe we should turn back." Then slowly a line of muskets emerged from the ship's side, but still there was silence save for the waves crashing against the vessel's barnacle covered timber.

"Are you sure that these folks are your friends?" Rod asked.

George frowned, "they were the last time I spoke to them."

"When was that?" Rod replied.

"A year ago," George replied.

Rod smiled, "hell that's enough time to fall in love, dump her and then say that the baby ain't yours." He smiled, death really meant little to him, but he noticed George begin to shake, what if they had found out that he had taken the prince's money as well as theirs.

Then a rope was hurled out from the side, Rod caught it and pulled the boat towards the ships side as a rope ladder fell from the ship's side. George at last exhaled and reached out for the ladder before pulling himself up, he almost twisted the rope ladder around and fell back into the boat before he felt the black man's hands shove his backside up. George climbed up, gazing back up the river towards London, half expecting the royal navy to come steaming down with all guns blazing before he tumbled over onto the ship's deck and panted like a foxhound after the hunt. Rod climbed up before looking back down towards the oarsman, "ain't you coming?"

"No, I ain't, I'm staying here! I don't trust foreigners."

George looked up from his panting to see a face that he knew from a hundred pamphlets: Hugo Chaval. Chaval was a large built man with a head of wiry black and broad smile on his tanned face, "what are you doing down there *Camarada?*"

George rose slowly and brushed himself down, and tried to look again the person he made himself out to be, the leader of the free British. Chaval cut an exotic figure that night on the Thames, a character from a novel brought to life. "General," George bowed slightly.

Chaval laughed, "you still speak no Spanish? English is the language of the imperialists!"

"And Spanish ain't?" Rod grunted.

George ignored him. "I am learning," he lied. "It is good to see you after all this time. You took a great risk coming here."

"To meet you I was prepared to face the devil's own navy!" Chaval's eyes then crossed and climbed to Rod, "who is this?'

"This is my friend Rod."

"He looks like my grandfather," Chaval lied.

"Really?"

"Yes, of course," Chaval started as he lead George towards his cabin, "there is much African blood in my veins as there is the land Veneagua." He then leant over and hissed, "he is a North American?"

"Yes," George replied.

"I have to be careful the North Americans will be anything to kill me!" Chaval gazed back at the huge black shadow following them.

"You do not have to worry about that one, he is an old friend of mine," George lied.

Chaval pushed his way into the captain's cabin, which was a grand affair, as befitting a captain in his Hispanic majesty's service. Chaval sat behind the great mahogany table with relish before brutishly resting his boots on it's polished surface. George made his way straight for the spirits and descended like a seagull on the box of cigars he was offered, he would have stuffed two in his mouth at the same time if he knew he would have gotten away with it. "It is good to know that there are still British people like you."

George wanted to reply but he had his mouth full of Chaval's chocolates.

"You know my friend, once a man like me, an *Indio* would only have entered a place like this to clean it, now I sit here as it's master!" Chaval boasted. "The North Americans hate to see a man like me as a leader, because they are killing their own natives as fast as they can, within a century they will be as Carthage is now, people you only read about in history books." Chaval's eyes were distant and moistened.

George helped himself to the rum and laughed, "well what can you do?"

"These people are our brothers," Chaval continued, "we are the same north and south, one people, true Americans, not vagrants from the slums of Europe! The Spanish were cruel and enslaved us but the Yankees are driving us into extinction!" Chaval then began to croon some Spanish ballad.

Rod shook his head, another dickhead.

You didn't need to understand Spanish to know that Chaval's song was a sad one, he then held the last note before he sighed. "Let us hope that the discontent in Britain can find it's way to power, because your country is the key link in the coalition of evil!"

"The place is seething with discontent; it is like a lake of oil that just needs a match," George enthused.

George was about to say something else when Chaval started to croon another sad ballad, that was as pathetic as a Portuguese fado song, neither of his guests knew where to put themselves. Chaval then shrugged, "I do not know why the

British and the colonists are such friends now, they were enemies from the start. The colonists do not like them, just like no slave looks fondly back on his master, especially if they were not given their freedom but had to kill for it."

"The British people are being betrayed!" George declared, "and they'd better wake up before it's too late."

"Are you the man to lead them though George?" Chaval smiled.

"Yes of course! Who else is there?"

Chaval then leant back, " if I help you into power there is something I want."

"What is that?"

"The Malvinas islands," Chaval smiled.

George frowned, "the Malvinas?"

"You might know them as the Falkland islands," Chaval smiled.

"What the hell do you want them for?" George replied.

"We want to liberate them," Chaval smirked.

"Liberate what?" George frowned, "there are only sheep there! Why don't you liberate a place where people actually live?"

Chaval nodded and then pointed to a map of the Americas, from Mexico to the Tierra del Fuego, "you know what that is a map of?"

George shook his head, "no."

"That is a map of Latina America," Chaval smiled and then drew back, "Latina! America!" He then shouted and brought his fist down on the desk, "latina!" He then brought out a stick and pointed to pink parts of the map, "Latina America, then what is that? The Malvinas! Belize! Guyana! Jamaica! Trinidad! What the hell are those places? Trinidad for God's sake, even the name is ours. These pink parts of the map should go!"

"And what of the people there?" George frowned.

"I don't know! They can swim back To England or die! Latina America will be one country with one language, Spanish!" Chaval shouted.

George then drew back, and his mouth gaped open, how had he not seen it before but Chaval was just another imperialist, no different to Prince Anthony, in fact if anything worse? How could that be? "What about Brazil?" George murmured.

Chaval waved that way, "Portuguese is just Spanish not spoken correctly, the Brazilians will learn to speak correctly,don't worry about that"
"And what if they don't want to?" Rod asked.

Chaval ignored the question, "oh I have seen a country, a land so vast, from California to Patagonia"

"Could you supply me with arms?" George murmured.

Chaval then began to croon again, and he smiled as if he was singing to his sweetheart, looking into George's eyes so that he blushed. Chaval then frowned, "for what? For you to cause a distraction whilst we take the Malvinas?"

"No I want to liberate Britain," George replied softly.

"Liberate?" Chaval frowned, "how can you liberate them? The British are the oppressors."

"But people are people Hugo," George replied.

Chaval stopped and just frowned for a moment , as if he hadn't understood, "do you really think so?"

"Yes," George tried again.

"Well I don't!" Chaval snapped.

Chapter Six:

Does anyone really believe in anything anymore? The bishops in their miters who stride into their vast cathedrals do they believe in God? If there was any money in Buddhism they would be opening up temples instead.

Most people would have said that Prince Tony believed in nothing, but Sunday morning saw him and his large mouthed wife march into church without fail. Tony threw his shoulders back as he paraded like a peacock into Westminster abbey and he looked down at the congregation with contempt. They had voted for him but he hated them, Britain was finished and they were too stupid to know it. The thing that got him is when things were going bad, when it was obvious that he was up to no good still they didn't turn on him, just as long as a Briton has money in his pockets he doesn't care. That is why Tony hated them, at least an Irishman was prepared to make himself poor for his country, a Briton wasn't. Usually if he just came out and made some glib speech and laughed at them they were happy! Mind you it helped that he had had a line of 'opposition' leaders who were either as stupid or as dirty as he was. He felt more like an emperor than a prime minster as he walked down the middle of the abbey, where kings and saints were buried. This was conquered land for him, it was a foreign church, despite his posh accent he was a Scot, and like George his father had bred in him a hatred for the English, but because he spoke like them they never got it. There was something bizarre and un-natural about the man, his cabinet sat hunched over in their pews and watched like smacked dogs as he passed. They knew he was no good but they had been out of power for so long, they were so hungry to rule that they would accept anyone who won and he was a winner. His arrogant contempt almost looked like piety and at least it meant he never had that inane grin of his. Tony strolled down the aisle before heading out to where the clergy usually only sat, he said he liked to be alone in church and they had arranged for him his own chapel where he could have some privacy.

The minute Tony entered the room his joker's grin returned, "bloody hell bound heretics a curse on you all!" He spat back, his eyes then fell on his wife, "come on let's go to a real church."Tony then headed out through a door and into a lesser carriage, his wife had entered and had only just sat down when he closed all the blinds and the carriage took off.

"You're losing money in this job," she snapped.

"Maybe, but I will be out of it soon," Tony smiled, "the longer I spend in it the more contacts that I am making, and the more jobs I will have when I leave power. But it isn't just about money, I am doing God's work, first in attacking the schismatic Servs and now here in England. After I have finished the church of Rome will not be the second but the first church of the country, we will have gotten back what was stolen from us all those years ago: England!"

"And Wales," his wife added.

"Who gives a toss about that?" Tony replied, "the only thing that place is good for is voting for us, their votes keep us in power, but if the Holy Father ever came here don't think that he would bother going there."

The carriage headed out of Westminster and into London's poorest area, his eyes crossed the slums, as he peered out through the blinds, these were the people who had voted for him because his party was the party of the poor but he had betrayed them. There was no work about, but still the boats came with more and more people and they ended up here, there were no houses left in the capital now, to buy one you needed to be a millionaire. His wide mouthed wife leant forwards, "you know my love, I never understand why you hate these people so much, I mean everyone knows why I do, my family are Irish, but I never got it with you."

Tony's eyes were distant he then smiled again, "I have my reasons."

The carriage squeezed up a back alley, then it's door opened and Tony nervously looked out before stepping out. This was where the church of Rome, the church of the last pope standing, lived in London, in a squalid back alley. On the map of Christianity Rome is no more important than Madras where Saint Thomas died and is buried, and the Romans were the ones who killed the Messiah, but to Tony the Roman church was the only church.

As the Prince entered the old Irish priest edged back, he was afraid that all this was a trap, that Tony was only toying with him, that he would one day come with soldiers and take them all away, but couldn't he send henchmen to do this? Why did Tony come himself? Rome had sent messages to him themselves to say that this heretic was to be received and treated as one of the faithful. There was something else about him though, he could sense the evil in him, this man had no place in church.

Tony entered this church more humbly and bowed towards the altar before closing his eyes in prayer. The priest tried to carry on with the service but he could almost hear Tony's thoughts as he prayed but it felt like he did not pray to heaven but to hell. The congregation still looked at him with fear, he was not fashioned from the same clay that they were.

Tony's eyes then opened and he sat back and watched the service with that sinister smile of his slowly rising into a broad grin. He had favoured this church, the others had suffered at his hands. The Pope of Alexandria had visited England recently and he had been received here more or less well, he even started saying that other church leaders were not right when they complained of being poorly treated here. However when the Pope had been leaving he had been made to take off all his clothes and had been humiliated. The border guards had said that they had been looking for weapons and then had confiscated his large, gold cross. Tony had only been sad that he had not been there to see it himself. The Prime Minister's eyes settled on a statue of the Messiah, and as the priest's old Irish brogue grated the statue changed. Jesus's skin bled red and horns sprouted from his head, before his skull turned towards his servant and Tony looked into the eyes of satan. The statue's lips them moved: "I want more deaths, more sacrifices, more wars, more hatred."

"Yes I will do so my sire," Tony murmured.

"What did you say?" His wife leant forwards.

"Oh nothing my dear," Tony replied as the statue became a statue again and a depiction of Jesus stared benevolently back at him.

At the end of the service Tony got to his feet and walked up to receive communion, the priest tried not to meet his eyes. "It is good to see you here again my son," the priest lied.

"Thank you Father," Tony then turned and looked over the crowd of Irish immigrants. "Today we meet here in this humble place," he looked about at the clumsily made pews and hastily painted icons, and he nodded, his lower lip bulged out, "but one day we will hold our services in Westminster Abbey!"

He expected them to cheer but they only looked afraid, a lot had come here to get away from the 'troubles,' the last thing they wanted was to meet another war monger. There was an awkward silence. Tony then nodded before striding out, "you shouldn't have done that," his wife hissed, "that is a church not a council chambers."

"Your people seem harder to sucker than English people, a group of northern idiots would have lapped that up." Tony then smiled, "I just wanted them to know that their prayers will be answered one day."

As the door closed one of the congregation spoke in broad County Donegal, "why in the name of sweet Jesus do you let that man in here?"

The priest smiled weakly, "the church is for everyone Kieran, you know that, besides it's his country not ours."

Tony sat back in his carriage and looked at his wife, no one could say she was pretty, no one could say she was kind, but she had one quality that he loved, she was as twisted as he was. "Great Britain," he mocked, "well I think that it is less great now isn't it?"

They weren't returning to the abbey, it was too late now, one of his men would have made his excuses, important government business was the usual one. The coach took a different road which passed the globe and Tony peered out through the blinds and his eyes settled on Dumfries's name: "I wonder what his game is?"

"Who?"

"George Dumfries."

"I don't know why you don't have that man shot," his wife stuffily replied.

The prince drew back, "you might be right but I do not know about him, he seems to be trying to tell me with this new venture of his that he is an idiot, no one to worry about."

"Well, what is wrong with that?" The wide mouthed woman replied.

"I don't like being told things, I like to find things out for myself, if he is telling me that he is a fool then maybe it is because he isn't!" Tony then sank back, "I will have to keep my eye on him, maybe I will have a word with my mentor. Maybe he can clear the waters for me."

"Who do you mean, your mentor?"

Tony smiled, "the man who I met while I was still at university, the man who got me to go into the worker's party, at first I thought he was crazy, I have never worked in my life, but he said if I followed what he said I would be rich beyond my dreams. I did what he said and now I am here, everything that he said would happen happened." Tony then banged on the carriage roof, "driver, the palace of Westminster!"

The small coach which looked as if it came form the lower classes was stopped until the Prince's head appeared through the blinds, then the sentries staggered back in fear, "sorry your Highness, "in a body they sank to their knees.

The carriage swept past them, "plebs," Tony sneered before the coach pulled up and he got out and turned to help his wife down and then gave the guard who met them an order to get them a new carriage.

"Where are we going?" his wife asked.

"To see my mentor," Tony grinned.

The palace was empty, but Tony looked up to the line of ravens and he knew Pantsdown was there. Slowly they walked up the same steps that George had a few nights before. It was then that the wide mouthed woman drew back, "we're going to see Pantsdown aren't we?"

"Yes," Tony grinned.

"This guy gives me the creeps," she shuddered.

"I don't know why, everything we have is thanks to him, if it wasn't for him I'd still be a barrister trying to scrape by on a few hundred thousand pounds a year, living in some town house down in that slum of Chelsea." Tony's hand gripped hers tightly, "you must be one of the few people in the country not to like him. He was always more popular than me."

"Yes but nobody much voted for him," she replied.

"That wasn't his fault, no one votes for the Whigs anymore," Tony replied.

Tony lightly tapped on the door. "Please come in," came a friendly voice on the other side and he looked at his wife and gave a smile before pushing open the door. Pantsdown stood in a dressing gown by the fire, "ah Tony how nice it is for you to come to see me, and you have brought your charming wife Charnae how are you?"

"Fine," she smiled stiffly.

"Well I do seem rather popular of late," He smiled.

"What do you mean?" Tony asked.

"Oh don't you know?" Pantsdown smiled, "I had the theatre world's newest star out here the other night, George Dumfries."

Tony stepped inside and closed the door behind Charnae, "what did he want?"

"Oh he came storming in here like Robert the Bruce talking about insurrection and rebellion," Panstdown smiled, "I didn't know if it wasn't part of his new comedy act."

"That's what I can't figure out as well," Tony replied, "I mean I have it on good authority that he is working for us, but then I know he is getting paid by Kestrel as well."

"It is so hard to be monogamous these days," a glint shone in Pantsdown's eye. "Oh how I miss those days when we were in government together."

Charnae frowned, "but you were never in government, you were in another party."

Pantsdown feigned shock, "oh crumbs I forgot."

"There is no such thing as parties now dear, you know that," Tony guided his wife into a chair and hoped she wouldn't open her wide mouth and embarrass him again.

"I don't care what party I am in, just as long as there is enough wine there," Pantsdown smiled and reached for a bottle, "would you like some?" The former leader of the Whigs then poured out three glasses, "this wine is OK, it isn't Servian," with that he laughed.

"Oh yes quite, they would poison it if they knew you were getting it," Tony smiled.

"Oh they were alright with me once, you know I remember going there to Servia, and some stupid priest showed me around one of the old monasteries, oh it was beautiful not one corner of it was without some kind of painting. Have you ever been inside one of those churches?"

"Only after it has been burnt down I'm afraid," Tony confessed.

"It might have been this one, anyway the priest was explaining to me in his heavily accented English and I was nodding, and saying how beautiful it was, but all I was thinking was how it would look on fire, you know flames creeping up around the faces of Jesus and Moses and whoever else was there. Then I looked at the priest and imagined him on top of a bonfire, like an effigy of dear old Guy Fawkes. God knows whatever happened to that priest, no doubt he was burnt to death , in his church they probably made a saint out of him now." Pantsdown then offered the wine out, "so I guess everyone is happy, he became a saint, the people living there have a nice, romantic ruin to clamber over instead of a boring old church, and the colonists got the war that they were after."

"What about George?" Tony asked sipping at his wine.

It was as if Pantsdown had not heard the question, "you know I am from the north of Ireland, my father was a protestant, and my mother a catholic, do you know what I learnt from that?"

"No," Charnae asked.

Pantsdown then drew back, "from my father I learnt to hate the Catholics, and from my mother I learnt to hate the Protestants, so I hated everyone there. You know when I was in Servia I hated them there too."

"Why? They had never done anything to you," Charnae replied.

"Oh no, they have never harmed one hair on the head of anyone from these shores, but I find with hate I can just turn it, I can hate anyone for any reason."

"So what about George?" Tony tried again.

Pantsdown sat down and thought, "I'll tell you what leave him to me. I'm going to call his bluff, I'm going to say 'alright George I am with you, let's take power!' Then let us see what he does, although he doesn't look like the sort I would go into war with, he looks like the kind you'd raid a tuck shop with."

Tony laughed, "alright, thanks Patrick." He then smiled, sipping at the wine, Charnae tipped hers into a cactus plant, it looked too much like blood to her.

Pantsdown nodded, "you know Tony this is the side that no one ever sees about you."

"What do you mean?"

"Well most world leaders would just shoot George and dump him into the river, but you are giving him a chance to show his colours."

"Before I have him shot and dumped in the river," Tony laughed.

"Yes quite so."

It was Sunday afternoon when Rod and George climbed off the rowing boat and walked back towards the Globe. "So there we are Rod," George enthused, "you have met one of the greatest men in the world today."

"Who?"

"General Chaval!" George replied, "he is one of the great world leaders, a man who stands up to the colonists and looks them in the eye and says-"

"He looked flakey to me," Rod cut in.

"Flakey? What do you mean by that?"

"He looked like he wasn't shuffling a full deck," Rod replied.

George looked at him, "you really don't get it do you?" In his heart though he was disappointed, there is a point where the left of politics and the right meet and look the same that is where Chaval was.

"I mean why should every one in the Americas speak Spanish?" Rod continued, "I mean that ain't an American thing is it?"

"Alright, I get it," George snapped.

"All those guys in power are like the slave masters, it don't matter if the boss is in Alabama speaking English or a Frenchie down in New Orleans, he is still the same kind of bastard. You know the worst kind though?" Rod asked.

"No."

"The black guy, the freed man who goes into the slave trade himself, he is a right proper bastard, they beat their blacks as bad as anyone, they forget where they come from. Chaval is like that, maybe his momma was poor and working out in the fields, but his wife ain't, and his daughter won't, they ain't one of us anymore, they are one of them."

George nodded, maybe Rod was right at that, "maybe." He would have to find someone else to help him in his rebellion.

They entered the theatre again, as if they had only been gone an hour, Princess Rula rushed to George, "how are you George, we were all worried about you?"

"Oh we weren't gone that long were we?"

"Yes you were," a voice came from behind him, it was Enver Mull, he was still dressed like a clown but his face was that of a hard businessman. "Where were you?"

"Oh just had to go somewhere," George replied casually.

Then Slyface emerged from Mull's office, "and where's Rupert?"

"Rupert?" George frowned.

"Yes my associate," Slyface snarled.

"He must be talking about that dude who-" Rod started but George cut in:

"What the blond fellow?"

"Yes," Slyface's mouth puckered, "the blond fellow."

"That dude went for a swim," Rod cut in.

"What? In the Thames?" Slyface gasped, "that's only fit for rats to swim in, it would kill anything else."

"I think that he had had a wee dram," George grinned.

Slyface nodded, he had only just learnt that phrase, "sounds like it."

Enver then looked sternly at George, "you should not have left the theatre, you had another song to sing. The audience went away disappointed, and that they should never do."

"Well we all get disappointments in life," George started and his face arched in a smarmy smile.

Mull coldy cut in, "you will have to lose some of your rights."

George took out a fresh Havana cigar, drew it under his nose first before planting it between his lips. Mull strode over and snatched the cigar, "you will lose some of your privileges for start, first thing to go will be the cigars."

Broadmoor smiled and took out his own cigar and lit it before wafting the smoke in George's direction.

Slyface looked at George, "we'll find Rupert.'

"Yes you do that," George snarled and his eyes followed Slyface out, waiting until the door had closed before he turned to Mull. "I thought you said that this kind wouldn't dare set foot inside the Globe."

"Well I lied!" Mull replied, "you know what one of those are don't you? You're a politician after all!"

George smarted, he felt like punching the over flowering daisy, Rula walked over and slid her arm around her waist, "it's alright George."

"Thank you sweetheart," George replied. His eyes burnt as they watched Mull go back into his office, "I want to get even with those responsible for me having my rights taken away from me!"

"You've no one to blame but yourself George," Broadmoor started, "you knew the commitments this show demanded before you entered it."

"I bet there ain't a drop of liquor left in my dressing room now," Rod moaned.

"Yes this bastard will have drunk it all," George's eyes leveled on Broadmoor, and he vowed that if he was successful and toppled Prince Tony the first thing that his new people's government would do is to put that long legged freak against the wall and have him shot.

Chapter Seven:

George didn't know what was worse, not being allowed to have a cigar or watching Broadmoor with his, and he seemed to smoke one after another. George paced like a caged lion and kept repeating "I'm going to get even with those responsible for me having my rights taken away from me!"

Chester sat and watched him and shook his head, "is he really in parliament?"

Broadmoor smiled, "yes."

"But he can't win an argument."

"That's why he's in the smallest party in parliament," Broadmoor smiled.

"How many are in it?"

"Just one, him," Broadmoor head just tilted back in laughter, "imagine him in government, he'd have to be everything, Home Secretary, Foreign Secretary and Minister for Administrative Affairs. He'd be giving orders to himself."

George couldn't hear what they were saying but he could guess. Rula sat next to him, "you don't want to listen to them, one is just a baby and the other is crazy."

George winked at her, "thanks love." He then got to his feet and headed over to Mull's office.

"Where's he gone?" Rod asked.

"He's got to nominate."

"Nominate?" Rod frowned, "what the hell is that?"

"Every week we get to decide who to throw off the show, I mean what cast member, we don't like."

"Well there's no need to guess who he will choose," Rod noted.

"Well there's no need to guess who you will choose," Mull echoed Rod's words as George closed the door.

"Yes," George replied, sitting down, "Rula!"

"Rula?!" Mull gasped, "you two are friends."

"Me? Friends with a clingy bitch like that! I hate her conversation, posh bitch." George then mimicked her voice, "'Mama and Papa lost all their lands in Poland when the nasty Prussians invaded.' Who cares? So now you are the same as the rest of us, she's a bloody immigrant like my grandfather was, whatever they had in Poland is all gone now!"

"I thought that you would pick Broadmoor," Mull replied.

"No, why should I? He is someone who rose up from the streets, not some castle in, wherever it was, Pomerania or Pomegranate, some bloody place that I have never heard of anyway, where no doubt the land is dirt cheap anyway. I'm glad the Prussians took it away from them!"

"So is that really your nomination?" Mull asked again.

"Yes," George confirmed, "get rid of the bitch, she may have been pretty in her day but that was a few centuries back now. I don't know whether you lined her up for me, but I prefer my meat a little more tender. I don't know where you found her."

"She's famous, even in the colonies people know her."

"Then send her over there, hopefully the boat will sink on the way!" He then strode out, the anger fleeting from his face in an instant to be replaced by a sickly smile as headed straight over to her, "hello sweetheart, what's been going on since I have been in there?"

"Nothing really, Broadmoor's been smoking a lot, I don't know where he gets it all from."

"Mull gives him the cigars, and he has been starving me," the hatred returned to his eyes.

"Don't you think they are doing it deliberately for you two to hate each other?" Rula asked.

It was as if he hadn't heard her, "I'll get even with him though." He then smiled, "they really are a bunch of idiots, since I've been in here no one has asked me if I know the Prime Minister, what's he like all that. They don't really care, or maybe they are just too ignorant."

"Yes the one girl over there when I said you from Dundee she thought that it was in Wales," Rula added.

George grinned, "that says it all." He went to get another cigar and of course he found that he didn't have any and cursed.

After the last person had gone into his office Mull came out, and looked over the cast. George had gotten the most votes, everyone wanted him gone apart from Rula and Rod but Mull's eyes instead shifted onto Chester: "Sorry kid it's you." "What?" Chester stammered, "how can that be?"

"No there's something wrong here," Broadmoor shook his head, "this is like one of those elections that George wins in East London."

"What's that supposed to mean?" George snarled.

Before an argument could erupt though Mull cut in, "oh and by the way, George voted for Rula."

A silence fell over the theatre, even Broadmoor's big mouth closed as Rula turned to George with eyes filled with tears, "is that true George?"

George looked at her without shame, "yes it is, I am sick of you." He then turned around and headed back to his dressing room. He caught the stage hand's eye as he went passed him but couldn't hold his stare for long.

Rula seemed to be in shock for a time, she trembled before bursting into tears, she then felt a hand on her shoulder, she turned around and saw Broadmoor, "don't worry about it, he's a grade A, 100%, completely genuine wanker, you're not to blame, they broke the mould after they made him and threw it away so there couldn't be anymore."

Vile then stepped forwards, "you know who he reminds me of? Garibaldi, of course I met him when I was in Italy and I said-"

Broadmoor turned on Vile, "will you shut up you old fool?"

"That's what Mozart said to me when I-"

"Well why don't you then?" Broadmoor cut in.

Chester packed his bags, Broadmoor watched him, "you know I still think that George got the most votes."

Chester shrugged, "doesn't really make much difference now does it."

George sat in his dressing room and looked into the mirror, he was beginning not to like the face that stared back at him. The door opened and George was about to tell whoever it was to get lost until he saw it was Rod, stood there like the judge on the last day: "What do you want?"

Rod shrugged, "that was a pretty bum thing you did out there you know that?"

George looked at him and nodded, "well I guess no one is perfect." He then looked away, Rod paused for a while before leaving. The door opened again and George was about to say that Rod was right and that he would apologize to her, but it wasn't him, instead his eyes met a small African man, little taller than a pygmy: "Who are you?"

"Alves."

George frowned, "what do you want?"

The African bowed slightly, he was nervous coming here, but he had to, "I have heard a lot of what you say Sir, and you are wrong."

"Who sent you the Prince?" George smirked.

"No the bones of my people sent me, their ghosts spoke to me in my dreams to come here," Alves drew forwards.

George got to his feet, "who let you in here?"

The black man continued,"real history isn't the kind that appears in books Sir. When you speak in favour of Kestrel you throw your lot in with a devil. He is from that breed of people who belong to nowhere, who have no king and no pope, they sail from one land to another and destroy what they find, like locusts."

"What are you talking about Fidel sent soldiers to Africa to help drive out the whites?"

Alves shook his head, "no Sir, they did not. I was there, I was fighting the Portuguese on the ground, the Muscovites sent us muskets. We used those muskets to drive the Portuguese out, but we were betrayed, the Portuguese had already signed a pact with Havana, they had not even left the country when Kestrel's bandits entered and declared war on us. They attacked the army of the north and then the south, and then when they had driven them back they started to kill us. There was a group of us who believed that the country's riches should be in the hands of it's people, and divided evenly. It was a rich land, we could have all been living like kings now but Kestrel didn't want that, he wanted the black oil which ooses out of Kabinda like syrup, he wanted it to sell it to the colonists."

"The colonists," George frowned, "you are joking, Fidel is their chief enemy, enemy number one. He never has any dealing with them."

Alves shook his head, "no it is a lie. Kestrel put his stooges in power and they sold the oil to the colonists and the gold they gave him in return then paid for his soldiers who came over to kill us. Colonist gold paid for it all, everything you see in Havana today was paid for with money stolen from us." The African's face then became distant and he remembered back to one May night. "I remember the night Fidel's men came to kill our leader Nito, they killed not just him, but his pregnant wife, his friends, anyone who had anything at all to do with him. They killed thousands of us, and it is true our own people turned on us, people who were my friends only the day before were tracking us down to kill us."

"No doubt they had their reasons."

"Their reasons were they were scared of Kestrel's thugs and Kestrel wanted to rob our country. They killed us because we wanted to help the poor. I was lucky to escape with my life."

George smiled, "yes that old story."

"Later the man he put in power Augustus began to look at his hands and lament the blood on them, he no longer had the stomach for more killing, so the Muscovites killed him, he went into one of their hospitals and never came out of it. Then they put a foreigner in power, a man as black as I am but he speaks no African language. Some people say that he is an American slave that Kestrel bought to do his bidding, others that he escaped from the plantation island of Sao Tome. But one thing is for sure, he hates our people with a passion, I reckon he was one of those children who arrive in our country and grows up with us but is never one of us."

George drew back, he could have been talking about him, for a moment he was haunted by the story, then his old arrogance returned to his face, "bullshit."

"Sorry?" Alves frowned.

"Bullshit, balderdash, bunkum, baloney," George smiled, "take your pick."

"Sorry?"

"What you just told me, it's nonsense or lies, who is paying you?" George drew forwards, "the imperialists?"

Alves looked him not just in the eye, but into his soul, "you are the imperialists. We had it! We had won! We had driven them out! Then your friends came and we lost it all again." Alves looked hard at George, but he could see that his eyes glazed and there was no breaking through it, he then withdrew and closed the door behind him.

George looked at the door and then shook his head, "liar," he muttered. In his heart though he knew the man was telling the truth, he had heard stories like that before, and yet he had to believe in Kestrel, if he did not believe in him then he had nothing to believe in. Then he thought about the night that he had met the butcher, or had he? Maybe that had been a dream?

Mull then came in, "who was that?"

"I don't know some African vagrant," George replied.

"You mean you didn't know him?"

"No I never and he should never have gotten close to me, I have a lot of enemies, you will have to improve security here," George ordered.

"Yes, of course George, but what did he want?"

"Oh you know these foreigners with their stories about voodoo priests and all that," George scoffed, his eyes met those of the stage hand as he peered into his room. George sent his boot against him, "and sack him as well will you, I am sick of his staring at me, I think he is weird or something."

Outside Rula dried her tears, "I think people will start to see through him now."

Broadmoor smiled, "maybe, maybe not, sometimes people like him have the world fooled for years, but he will get his comeuppance one day I am sure about that."

George could hear their voices, he knew that bitch would turn on him, he was right not to have trusted her. He then walked over to the window to where Slyface walked with another man who looked like his boss, no doubt they were investigating the blond man's disappearance. The second man then turned his face and George saw who it was with a smile, Leyte. The door opened and Rod came in, George smiled, "come here my friend, I have someone or rather something to show you."

Rod walked over, "what is it?"

"That man there with our government friend, you know who he is?"

"No."

"His name is Marcus Leyte and he is the worst type of creature who now scurries over the Prince's Britain. He was a journalist, reporting the war against Servia, of course he said everything the government wanted."

"Like what?"

"Many people died there, in one place they burnt a carriage and everyone inside it, we did it the British, later we said it was an accident that we hadn't meant to burn the carriage only the bridge it was crossing. It was a lie but thanks to Leyte we got away with it. He reported one thing after another wrong, so much so that after the war he had to leave his job. Then he got this one working for the government, maybe as a reward, maybe he was working for them all the time. That's how they get away with it all, a monarch who doesn't care, an opposition who don't oppose and a press who are bought and paid for."

"Do you think he's onto us?" Rod asked.

'Onto you," George thought, after all it was Rod who had thrown Blondie into the river, he had done nothing. George drew back, "who can say? He is only a disappearance until they find a body."

"Will they find one do you think?" Rod asked.

George shrugged, "I doubt it, he will have washed out to sea by now, maybe he will come ashore on some beach, but they will think he was a mariner who fell over board." The Scotsman then smiled, "you know Rod London is nothing compared with the great European cities, in another country they would build some great building to impress the world here they are doing something different."

"What?"

"They are building two new cities to challenge for the title of second city, Birmingham and Manchester and they are such ghastly places that no Londoner will ever moan about his city again."

Leyte drew down near the water's edge and touched it as if it was some kind of sleeping potion , "they must have drowned him," his eyes flitted around to Slyface, "did anyone see him come out here?"

"Yes, Broadmoor, he saw George come out then Rupert and then that tall black man and none of them came back," Slyface replied.

Leyte nodded, "Rupert had a musket didn't he?"

"Yes."

The water was icy cold and dirty, as he drew his hand out he had to wipe it against his trousers to get the sludge off, a cruel smile then rose on Leyte's face, he got up as if to shout 'eureka!' "The musket must still be there!"

"How do you know?"

"Take a look in there," Leyte ordered.

"In there?" Slyface asked, "but it's freezing!"

"That can't be helped, take your shoes and socks off and roll up your trouser legs, come on man! Get in there!"

Leyte knew very well that the chances of him finding the musket were slim, but still he would bully Slyface because he could, that was the golden rule in the Britain of Prince Tony, if you could bully someone else you did so. He pretended to look along the shore, while Slyface slowly took off his shoes and socks, hoping that Leyte would find something before he had to go in there. Even if Leyte would have found something he would have kept it hidden until Slyface had gone for his dip. Slyface drew up his trouser legs with arduous slowness and looked at Leyte with begging eyes.

"Get in there man!" Leyte urged and then covered his mouth so that the agent could not see him smile. Gingerly Slyface lowered one foot into the water and cursed to high heaven. He then looked back, Leyte couldn't speak because he knew that he would laugh, but just flagged in Slyface deeper. He kept urging him forwards until the water was up at his knees.

"I can't see nothing in this water," Slyface shouted back, "it's too dirty!"

"Keep going man!" Leyte shouted and bit his lip, "keep going!"

Maybe it was because Leyte was urging it to happen so much but Slyface slipped on a greasy rock and fell into the water, disappearing for a moment before scrambling out like a terrified dog, running onto the shore again. Leyte staggered back, bursting into the theatre, roaring with laughter.

"I wish this guy was in the audience," Broadmoor looked towards him.

Leyte then hid as the door opened and Slyface came in looking like a soaked rat, "whatever happened to you ?" Rula asked.

"I fell in the river," Slyface's teeth chattered.

"Yes I can see that," Broadmoor nodded, "seems to be a habit with you government agent people."

George then emerged with a big, broad Cheshire cat grin, his eyes then met Leyte's hiding behind a prop tree. George nodded to him before retreating back inside his dressing room, leaving Rod to emerge and throw a towel at Slyface, "hey man this ain't no weather to go skinny dipping in."

Chapter Eight:

It was later that same day that the same humble carriage which had taken Tony to the catholic chapel drew up in front of the Globe Theatre, it's blinds down. The same driver stepped down and opened the door and then the Lord Patrick Pantsdown stepped down and looked at the theatre with a vague disgust. Hurriedly the driver rushed to open the door and Pantsdown entered with the air of a man who had lost his way to the opera.

Vile looked up and then walked over with his arms open, "hey Patrick my friend!" Of course they hardly knew each other, but no one ever said that to Vile, nothing could be worse to Pantsdown than to hug this walking lump of slime, but he offered out his hand which he shook, before spraying his hand with perfume afterwards.

"Are you Bruce Forsett?" The young blond bimbo asked.

Pantsdown just smiled weakly, he had hoped to enter here un-noticed, Broadmoor just nodded, Rula drew forwards and Pantsdown drew down to kiss her hand, "I am charmed."

"Who are you here to see?" Rula asked.

"George, I'm afraid."

Instantly she drew her hand back, "he's in there."

Pantsdown then headed to George's door, tapped on it briefly before drawing the door open quickly. It was something he always did, hoping to find someone with their knickers round their ankles. George was about to curse before he saw who it was and he got to his feet as if the pope had entered. "Lord Patrick."

Pantsdown nodded and raised his finger to his lips before looking at Rod and nodding towards the door. Rod frowned. Pantsdown nodded towards the door again before George got his meaning, "oh Rod could you leave us please? Lord Patrick wishes to talk to me of things of a personal nature."

Rod shrugged, "whatever." Rod then walked towards the door, glancing at Pantsdown before he left, "he looks like one weird son of a bitch to me."

Pantsdown smiled.

"I'm sorry about that," George ushered Pantsdown towards a seat.

"Oh it's quite alright, I guess he has some charm in an entirely ethnic way," Pantsdown then looked at the seat and placed a handkerchief on it before sitting down.

"What do I owe the honour for, I mean your visit?" George asked.

Pantsdown held up his finger to silence him before stalking over to the door, and drawing out a hat pin from his coat, he then bent down and jabbed the hat pin through the keyhole, drawing it back, and then nodding. He then smiled, "I always do that, if it comes back with blood on it it means someone is listening to us."

"I'm sure someone could lose an eye through that," George agreed.

"Yes well you shouldn't listen at keyholes, Jesus never liked people doing that!" Pantsdown nodded and sat down on his handkerchief again.

"So what do I owe the honour to?" George asked again.

Pantsdown smiled, "well I have been thinking about what you said last time." He then became the actor again and adopted that air of indignation that he had had in the past when he urged for the Servs to be driven off their land. When he had fought for the king he had learnt the language of the enemy, now he played at being a politician he had learnt their words as well. "You know the Whigs are not just another group of gravy trainers on the take, it is the country's oldest and most respected party. We have a tradition to live up to. Maybe we have become like an old water buffalo, that lolls about, eats and sleeps, and does little else, but we still have our horns, and can kill any hyena like Tony."

"What are you saying?" George urged.

"I am saying that I have an innate sense of fair sense," Pantsdown looked out of the window, "I forgot about that for a time and I should thank you for reminding me of that."

"So what are you saying?" George tried again.

Pantsdown's eyes settled on him, "I can no longer put up with what I see. I can no longer put up with colonists coming to London to give our Prime Minister his orders. Since when have they ever wanted anything good for His Majesty's Britannic Realm? What we have seen is one unjust war after another, against the Mesopotamians, we went in there because they had a secret weapon which would destroy the world! That's what Prince Tony said, he got up and declared that to all the world, but it was a lie! The Mesopotamians couldn't make a water bomb they are so backwards, we all knew it."

"I remember saying as much at the time," George said under his breath, "so what do you want us to do about it?"

Pantsdown drew back, "this man, this evil man has to go one way or another."

"We won't beat him at the ballot box," George agreed, "because he doesn't need a majority to win the elections."

"Then we won't use elections," Pantsdown smiled.

"Then what?"

Pantsdown then drew back, "when I went into fight the armies of the Sultan of Malacca I didn't wait for no vote. I was no normal redcoat who took the King's shilling and then stood in front of the Tsar's cannons. No I was a special soldier, we went into God forsaken jungle kingdoms where we were outnumbered one hundred to one. I have gotten rid of many Prince Tonys in my time, I've dragged some off their thrones myself, with my bare hands."

George nodded, it's funny people never wore gloves when they did such a thing, "so what are you saying?"

Pantsdown sighed and then ran his fingers back through his hair, "what I am saying George is that I am with you, together with my supporters and your people we have enough to get the Prince out of power and then we'll put him in court, he should answer for his crimes!" Pantsdown then got his feet and gripped his lapels. It was strange but George knew he was a rogue that he had been the one urging Tony into war in the first place, and yet he was sucked into it all. "He has blackened the good name of this country, made us ashamed to be British."

George nodded, even though Pantsdown was more Irish than he was, but he had purged it from every syllable, every inflection, "but if Tony goes won't another rogue just take his place?"

"Then we will get rid of him as well, we will get rid of them all until His Majesty has no choice but to give us power!" Pantsdown declared.

Now it was George drawing back, "but Tony has the army with him."

"Do you think they are enjoying his illegal wars, seeing their comrades die? If they see I am with you, they will be with you, they know that I am one of their own, that I risked my life as they risk their lives for their King. If it is a choice between me and Tony they will choose me every time." Pantsdown then drew back.

George nodded, "but we have no guns Patrick?"

Pantdown drew his finger to his lips again and then stalked over to the door and threw it suddenly open. On the other side Broadmoor and Rula looked back blankly, Pantsdown nodded, "just put some oil on these hinges, they seem fine now."

Pantsdown then drew back, "where were you going the other night when the spy vanished."

George replied without thinking, "Chaval had a boat moored off the Isle of Sheppey, I went out to talk to him."

Pantsdown tried to hide his satisfaction, "and what did he say?"

"He won't help us."

Panstdown nodded, and drew back, now he had enough to see George hang. "No he won't help us."

"He said that the colonists had plans to kill him," George added.

Pantsdown laughed, "of course they have, everyone has, even his friend Fidel Kestrel has plans to kill him, Chaval is living on borrowed time. He won't live long enough to help us."

"What about Kestrel then?" George asked.

Pantsdown smiled, "you still don't get it do you?"

"What do you mean?" George asked.

"We have to help ourselves, if I can get the guns, can you get the men?"

"Sure, if I go back to Castle Hamlet I will find enough men," George insisted.

Pantsdown nodded, "good, then I will see that you get the guns."

"But how?"

"First get out of this circus and go back to your people," Pantsdown then rose to his feet, "you know George I am the first Whig leader for a long time who is able to tell his people, go off and prepare for power!"

Rod watched Pantsdown leave and shook his head before launching himself forwards, tapping his knuckles against the still open door before drifting in, closing the door behind him, "who the hell was that?"

"That my dear brother Rodney was Sir the Lord Patrick Pantsdown, the most honourable well thought of man of principle in the land," George extended his hand after the dignitary.

Rod shook his head, "he looks like bad news to me."

George slammed the door shut, "there you go again, first Sir Jimmy Vile and now him? What is it with you? You don't like anyone we look up to in this country?"

"I know a sleaze ball when I see one," Rod replied, "and that guy wreaked of it."

"No this time you're wrong Rod, this man is a truly great man," George then gave a great eulogy.

Rod shook his head, "whatever man."

"You're wrong!" George jabbed his stubby little finger at him, "you're wrong! You're wrong! You're wrong!" George strode out and then he called the cast together, "brothers and sisters, I have an announcement to make."

George ran his hand through what was left of his hair, "I entered this house with the idea of spreading my message to a wider audience. But I have sat down and thought about it and I don't think it is working out. I don't think this is the right platform to express what I am about."

"I think it's the perfect place," Broadmoor muttered.

George heard him but ignored him, "so I think it is time for me to bow out."

Mull emerged, "you're leaving? But you have a contract!"

George smiled, "that my dear Mr Mull is not worth the paper that it is written on!"

Rod shook his head, "man I hope you know what you are doing."

"Yes I do Rod, the next few days will cement my place in history!" George then strode out.

Broadmoor looked at the door closing behind him, and then looked at the others, "well what do you make out of that?" He held out his hands in amazement, "what a prat! Conan the Librarian!"

Rod hesitated for a minute and then cursed before following him as he strode out into the street.

"Are you quitting too?" Mull shouted.

Rod never replied to him as George hailed a hansom cab down and climbed into it, Rod pulled himself up onto the side of it, "man you're making a mistake."

"What are you doing?" George gasped.

" I can't let you walk into a trap."

"What are you talking about?"

"That man, Pantsdown, he's baiting you a trap!" Rod pleaded. "Look if he's such a big shot what the hell does he need you for?"

"You don't even know what we talked about," George replied.

"I can guess. He's lying to you George!"
George shook his head, "what? He never tells lies, he must be the only man who don't, this is Sir Patrick Pantsdown we are talking about not some Gypsy vagabond."

"You're wrong George," Rod then shouted at the driver, "hey man, pullover!" The cab pulled to the curb and the big African jumped off. "You can go to your own funeral by yourself George I ain't having no part of it."

The cab pulled off again and George couldn't help but look behind several times but Rod never looked back at him as he walked back to the theatre. Normally George would have cursed him, but he couldn't this time, he knew Rod was a good man.

This time when he got back to Castle Hamlet it looked different. It was quiet, there was no crowd of well wishers waiting to see him come back. Only the hag was there washing her clothes. The carriage pulled up in front of the castle and George stepped out, "where is everyone?"

"They ain't here," the hag replied.

"Well I can see that but why?"

"You've gone too far this time George, you made a right proper Charlie of yourself up at that theatre, dancing around with ladymen and pretending to be a cat, people are sick of it. You are meant to be their man in the house of commoners not a circus clown."

George looked at her, "where are they all?"

"In the tavern."

George looked at the tavern and then strode over there, this wouldn't be easy but it was within his powers.

The tavern was packed as they gathered around to hear the opium dealer as he recounted of what he had seen in the Globe: "The one night I went there I saw him dressed up as a cat, the next night I see him dancing with a ladyman."

"With a ladyman?" The black smith asked laughing.

"Yes," the opium dealer nodded and the tavern erupted in laughter. He shouted over the top of it, "he was wearing some outfit that was so tight that you could see his lady pleaser and he's only got a little fella!" The laughter roared yet louder as the door opened and George entered. The laughter died slowly.

George nodded, "so this is where you all are."

"Where have you been George?" someone shouted, "we have missed you."

"I have been up west in London," George replied, he could see that this would be difficult but he carried on, "on important business."

"Is that what you call it?!" Someone shouted and the pub erupted again in hoots and howls again.

George ignored him, "I have been talking to Lord Patrick Pantsdown of the Whig Party, and he told me that we are to offer a united front. We have gone from being an army of hundreds to thousands brothers!" George looked across their faces, "now we as a family have to sit down and think about what we are going to do. Are we going to let history pass us by, are you going to go back to your ale or are we going to change this country! A chance like this may not come our way again!" George then looked over them, at least the smirks had gone, he nodded before he walked out.

George then walked back to his castle, crossing the drawbridge before pulling out the large, old key and fitting it into the lock. He didn't know if he had done enough, his speech had been short, maybe he should have talked more, it was hard to get it right. He didn't want to bore them, but his speech was hardly Henry V. What if when Pantsdown came back and there was no one backing him up? He could still hear Rod's voice telling him that it was a trap, but he blocked it out. He headed over to the liquor and poured himself a glass of rum, what did Rod know? He looked over the river again towards Kent, how many times had he thought that he was building something only for it to come crashing down? How many times would this happen? He was getting old, and what had it all been for?

He thought back to the day his grandfather had died, a long time ago now. He had lay there quite still for hours, something had gone wrong in his body and now he couldn't move, his eyes filled with terror, because in the end he had never believed in God, all those hours in church had been for nothing. Then his lips moved and George had edged closer, "what is it granddad tell me?"

Then his lips mouthed: "Bugger the English." Then his eyes closed and he was dead. If he had died with hate in his heart how could he have not passed through the gates of hell?

George heard voices and he headed around to the front of the castle, there was a window overlooking it, slowly he drew open the shutters and looked down on a small crowd, maybe fifty or so, but it was a start, George smiled:

"Thank you for coming brothers and sisters, I have seen the start of change in Westminster, the Whigs have come over to us already. We need to be certain of victory, we musn't lose through not giving it our best shot, that's why I want you to send the word out. Tell everyone you know in every part of this land to come here to Castle Hamlet! We are starting on a mission here, today the journey has started that will see us, the people in power!"

The crowd let out a cheer. "I don't want power," the hag coughed, "nobody ever wanted power here before you came."

From the shadows beside the tavern four eyes watched George, Leyte drew back and pulled the scarf down from his mouth, "well he's definitely getting ready for something. Should we make a move?"

From the darker shadows Pantsdown stepped forwards, "no, not yet!"

"But the guy is planning a rebellion!"

Pantsdown smiled, "yes I would say so." Pantsdown then turned around and headed away from the village.

Leyte pressed again, "Sir we should do something."

"We will wait, if we move now how many would we get? A dozen?" Pantsdown shook his head, "that is not good enough, give George some time to get more of them together."

"How long then? A week?"

"No, that might prove to be too long, you see my dear Mr Leyte, a rabble loses interest if you leave them too long, they find something else to do. No we will give it two days, that I think will give us enough time to collect the human effluence from London and the surrounding shires." Pantsdown then pulled open the door of his coach and he pulled himself inside, as soon as Leyte got inside he pulled down the blinds.

"You don't reckon it will turn violent do you?" Leyte asked.

"I doubt it," Pantsdown laughed, "they are relying on me to bring the guns."

Chapter Nine:

Two days passed, and Castle Hamlet swelled with more strangers, they came from London mainly, but a lot were from Essex as well. They were a mixed lot: People who hated the government, the country, the world, themselves. Amongst them however were others who believed in justice, who had seen through the lies the journals churned and the politicians spouted out, but hadn't yet seen through George. George united them all but it was no easy job. He looked out from the castle with a mixture of pride and fear, how could the Prince not notice this? He looked to see if he could see Leyte or Slyface, but he couldn't, but then maybe they had sent someone else, that would be logical. He had waited for Rod to come back, but he never did, maybe he wasn't ready to seize greatness or maybe he wasn't ready for suicide. He must have looked at that clock at least every minute, what if Pantsdown had not been serious? What if it had just been talk, would he still lead these people to London without guns? Or would he slink away, maybe back to Dundee? He had images of leading a great march on the capital with the march swelling in numbers with each milestone passed until it arrived in the capital as a tumult. Of course there were only a handful of milestones between here and Westminster.Then the doors of the palace would open like the rock on Ali Baba's cave and he would stride in and dictate to the king, or maybe he would just throw him off his balcony, that would send a message not just to the country but the world. What good was a king anyway who just sat back and let a scum like Tony rape his country?His eyes went from the clock to the window, and then about mid-day George closed his eyes and prayed for Pantsdown to come and then when his eyes opened he was there! Pantsdown appeared, walking through the crowd as if it was a street carnival. George rubbed his eyes to make sure he wasn't dreaming but when he opened them again he was still there, one man patted him on the back, "are you with us as well Patrick?"

"Oh yes, I am always on the winning side!" Pantsdown smiled before breezing into the castle. No sooner was he through the door when Dumfries burst forwards to meet him:

"Oh Patrick thank God you are here."

Pantsdown smiled, "what's the matter George? Don't you trust me?"

George weakly smiled, "you can't trust anyone in this kind of thing."

Pantsdown smiled, it was too late to think that, he thought. If George though walked outside and told everyone that it was all a joke or a mistake then he might save himself, but of course he knew that he wouldn't. "Are you ready then George?"

"Ready for what?"

Pantsdown laughed, "you came to me remember? The ship is here, let's get the guns!"

George hesitated, he still remembered Rod's words, he remembered the way this man had lied about the war in Servia, the way he had pushed Tony into his first war, how he had pushed the colonist's agenda, somehow though he pushed all that to the back of his mind, "yes come on."

The two leaders then walked out of the castle, "where are your people?" George asked.

"Oh they are waiting in London, I thought that it would be better if your people got the guns, they seem more capable of using them," Pantsdown smiled and lead them down to the river. George looked behind them, he counted at least two hundred people, but there had to be more, all marching behind him. He should have felt like a god but his heart was thumping wildly, as if he was heading to the gallows.

"So where is this ship?" George asked.

"There," he pointed to a fishing boat.

"It doesn't look much," George grumbled.

"There are over two hundred muskets in there," Pantsdown lied.

"Where did you get them from?" George asked suspiciously.

"The French, they are hoping to see one of their rivals bogged down in strife," Pantsdown smiled. "But we will take their guns and then turn them on them, with a proper leader we'll wipe their petty little empire off the map, and into the history books where every French endeavor always belongs."

George should have noticed that they were heading into long grass, he should have noticed the shadows creeping through it.

Pantsdown though kept talking, "you know the last battle I went into I was with Major Richard Sharpe, you ever heard of him?"

George nodded, "yes of course, they say he is a hell of a warrior."

"Nah," Pantsdown shook his head, "he's a chicken, how they make him look so good in those books I will never know, another one who is only good in books is Horatio Hornblower."

"He's no good as well?" George asked.

"No, he's a complete shower," Pantsdown replied.

Pantsdown's conversation distracted George so he didn't see the shadows creeping over the fishing boat. Some of his followers began to drop off, sensing the danger but only a few. But then Pantsdown never noticed the small rowing boat draw up beside the boat and a tall black man pull himself on board. Slowly Rod moved along it's deck, counting six of them, all with their sights trained on George. Rod's eyes settled on the one nearest to him, he then sank down and crept along the floor before hissing, "over here." Rod then darted back and waited for the man to come to him, and when he did, his eyes broadened before the big black man took his gun off him, "now get off my boat!" Rod nodded towards the starboard bow, "take a swim amigo." The man didn't argue for a long, he had never seen anyone like Rod, as he lowered himself down into the water Rod crept round to the others, "ladies, sorry to spoil your party."

George stopped before the boat, Pantsdown smiled, "come on let's take a look at the cargo." George hesitated, Pantsdown was all too cocky for his liking, he strolled up the gang plank, George gingerly followed. Pantsdown's smile sank though when he saw that the boat was deserted. "What the hell is going on?"

Rod then emerged with a musket in both hands, "I knew you were bad news the first time I saw you, you just smelt wrong."

George then got on board, "what's going on?"

"Your friend prepared for you a little trap," Rod smiled, "now go and call your men off, tell them no war today, you do the same George, say that everyone is now friends."

"I will do nothing of the sort," Pantsdown protested.

"Then you'll die, I wanted to kill you from the first time I ever saw you, you look like a slave master back in Dixie who lashed my back until it was raw, I never did get even with him over that." Rod's face iced with hate, "now do as I say, both of you."

George walked over to the port side, "brothers and sisters, there is no cargo, we have been let down, it is best we all go home."

Some tutted, and moaned, but most looked relieved, then the lions emerged from the long grass as thirty agents advanced with their muskets.

"Call your men off," Rod snarled, "else I'll blow your head off!"

Pantsdown hesitated before Rod slowly raised his musket and looked down it's long barrel to the politician's trembling face. "Stand down men! " Pantsdown ordered weakly.

"You what?" One of the agents shouted.

"Stand down!" Pantsdown shouted, before turning his back on them.

George's eyes then rounded on him, "so it was a trap."

"Didn't I tell you?" Rod snapped. "This guy was going to string you up."

Pantsdown lost his arrogant, amused smile, "now what?"

"The three of us are going on a little boat ride," Rod smiled.

"Please don't kill me," Pantsdown began to shake.

"Now come on, weren't you the one who use to be a warrior for the King?" George's old smile now returned.

"It's all been crap from the start," Rod snarled.

"What are you going to do with me?" Pantsdown glanced over to the shore, the two sides were heading off, he wanted to shout to them but he didn't doubt that that the black man would kill him.

"Let's just take that boat ride will we?" Rod replied.

"Do anything and the Prince will hunt you down," Pantsdown warned.

George smiled, "I don't think so, do you?"

Rod nodded, "you failed, I bet he don't like losers."

A lot of the old pompousness had now gone and for the first time for a long time Pantsdown was afraid. The boat headed down the Thames with Pantsdown at the wheel while Rod sank back in his seat and trained his musket on the honourable Lord's spine. "You know many slaves back there in the plantations dream of sitting where I am, with one of the great slave bosses before him, and all he has to think about is whether to kill him or not."

Pantsdown looked back, "I have never owned a slave." Only now was the Irish that he had fought so much to control creep back into his voice.

Now George's memory was coming back to him, "no Prince Tony gave you an entire country to enslave, he made you a viceroy there. A hundred churches fell into flame because of this man! People were driven from their homes, and the old people who were too weak or stubborn to move were butchered when this man's dogs came!"

"The Servs were mass murderers," Pantsdown replied.

"Then where are the mass graves? Our soldiers went in there but they didn't find thousands and thousands of dead did they?" George replied "like you said they would."

"They were invading other countries." Pantsdown tried again.

"That again is a lie, the borders of Servia have been drawing back, once it was an empire which stretched from the gates of Trieste into Macedonia itself! Now look at that same country, even the sacred soul of Servia, where it's monasteries were have been lost!" George found his old self, "we are the invaders, we the British, we are the mass murderers, not the Servs, not the Mesopotamians, but us! And it's all thanks to scum like you! Why did you push for that war so much?"

"I thought the Servs were wrong," Pantsdown tried again.

George snatched up another musket and aimed at the Lord, "don't lie to me man, else I'll kill you myself!"

"I had my orders, the colonists wanted a war, they wanted the Servs punished."

"Punished for what?" George asked, "they never did anything to us?"

"They weren't doing what they were told," Pantsdown's head sank, "you have to do what you're told these days. The colonists told me what to say, and I said it. There is that what you wanted to hear? So what are you going to do with me?"

"I say kill him," Rod replied coldly.

"That would make us the same as him," George replied.

"I don't care about that, I'll square it with Jesus when I get to heaven," Rod replied. "He sounds like the kind of dude that I can talk to."

Pantsdown then looked to the south where the Medway enters the Thames and beyond to the castle and cathedral of Rochester, and then he looked back at his captors: "Do you really think you can win George?"

"How do you mean?" George replied.

"The colonists have bought everyone, the King, the Prime Minister, everyone."

"They haven't bought me!" George replied.

"That makes you a black ant in the middle of a red ant colony, it is only a matter of time before they tear you apart," Pantsdown warned.

George smiled, "look I don't worry about things so much."

Pantsdown looked at him, "they own everything, there is nothing in Britain they don't own, every shire, every town, every village, it is all theirs!"

George smiled again, "this will all soon be over for you, we'll just go for a little boat ride."

"You don't get it do you?" Pantsdown snarled, "it's already over for me."

George was about to say something smart when suddenly Pantsdown made a break for it, bursting through the cabin door. Rod went to follow him but George grabbed him, he went some steps with George clinging onto him like a baby bear, before Pantsdown dived over the side of the boat. "Leave him!" George shouted, "let him go! He's finished anyway!"

They then watched Pantsdown struggle against the waves, "do you think he'll make it?"

George shook his head, "I doubt it, must be half a mile to shore." He then took the wheel and steered it away from him, "it always seems easy when you look at a map, oh I can swim that easy. I was in Wales once and it was a hot day, I thought that I would take a dip in the river Monnow, swim to the other side, I didn't get half way until I got into trouble, I don't know if it was cramp or just old age, but I nearly drowned there."

It was strange but George never looked back to see if Pantsdown made it or not, he wasn't interested, only a few days earlier he had praising him as one of the greatest people alive. Rod looked back but he could see nothing, "what if he does make it?"

"He will disappear, like a lot of people back in England. Like Robert Crook."

"Who?"

"Oh he went only a few days ago, he was in favour of Tony's blood thirsty war against the Servs as well, his was one of the chief voices demanding more and more blood. He wanted Servia wiped off the map of Europe forever, blown back to the stone age. However he was too vicious even for the Prince and he sacked him, I thought he would try to kill the scoundrel but instead Crook like Saint Paul came back as a man of peace. I was there in parliament when he made his great speech, they were weak points coming from him, he said how the war against Servia had been a legal one but this one was not. Of course both wars were illegal and unjust, it's just Crook had been crossed and when he was crossed he came out like a rabid weasel not thinking straight. The more he spoke, the deeper he dug his own grave. Tony'e eyes settled on him like a fat, black rat looking at a field mouse." George then paused and looked towards the grey horizon, remembering someone he had been friends with him once, they had both come from Scotland. They had drifted apart as Crook had been obsessed with money but he had never lost all his affection for him.

George smiled, "the rest I can only guess at. Crook had abandoned the long suffering woman he had been married to and married a younger, fresher vagina. They went on holiday to a mountain in the middle of nowhere, maybe he went willingly I do not know, but he and his young bride went up the mountain and only she came back alive. They were followed up there by four men, four men heading up a mountain no one ever went up. Who can say what went on up there? I'll wager Pantsdown will be heading up that same mountain."

Rod nodded, "that kind of thing goes on everywhere."

"It never use to much in England, that changed under Prince Tony, I could give you other names, tell you other stories but even here, out here in the Thames estuary with only you and me, even here I am afraid to mention those names."

Rod nodded, "so where to now?"

"First, we will get to France, we can't rest soundly until we are out of British waters, but even there we will not be safe. Colonist money has poisoned the French republic as much as it has here, it is no more the land of 'one for all and all for one,' it is now the land of me, me ,me. So we will go west."

Rod drew back, "to the colonies?!"

"No, not to the colonies, Havana, that is the only place we can go to now."

Rod drew back, "hell man, all these people are the same."

"Not Fidel Kestrel, he is the real deal," George affirmed.

"Yes like Pantsdown was." Rod then leant back and shook his head. "We need to take this boat to somewhere where there ain't no parliaments and no politicians as well."

To George that sounded like heading to hell, "where?"

"Back to the jungle," Rod replied, "I'd rather negotiate with hyenas and leopards than devils and *kimbandas*."

Neither knew much about sailing and they headed with luck into the English Channel and sailed down until they got to a forgotten place called Barneville, somewhere in Normandy. Night was sweeping in from the west, "we'd best find a port."

"Sure ain't no place there," Rod replied looking along the beach.

Then George raised the ship's telescope to his eye, "I can see something."

"What?"

A smile rose on George's face, "it's the good ship *Liberador.*"

Rod's face sank, "let it go man."

"I don't fancy sailing around here in the darkness," George replied.

"We'll find a harbor George, look we don't need them," Rod urged, but he could see that George's eyes were lost in madness. "We're in the English Channel not the middle of the Pacific, we'll head for Cherbourg, you can almost see the lights from here."

George shook his head, "no, it's our only hope, we need to get to that ship."

"No, George, look, forget about it," Rod urged.

George though ignored him and swung the wheel towards the great ship and back into his own personal madness. Rod drew back, and shook his head, maybe George was just one of those people who liked people who treated him badly. As they got near George headed out and started swinging his lantern and calling out: "Amigos, it's me George Dumfries."

There was silence again, but this time it was only seconds, the crew were braver here off the coast of France than they had been in the Thames estuary. The muskets appeared slowly as he continued to repeat his name until Chaval himself appeared and peered through the darkness, "*camarada* is that you?"

"Yes it's me!" George announced.

"What are you doing here?"

"I can't go back to England!" George shouted, "they'll kill me."

"Why?"

"I'll explain when I get on board!" George shouted.

Chaval looked at him, and then cursed to himself, before giving one of his sailors a signal. The rope ladder then tumbled down the side of the ship, and Rod took the wheel, "I'll steer the ship for you."

"But what about you?"

"I ain't going," Rod shook his head.

"But why?"

"I don't trust that guy," Rod replied, "I don't trust any of them, they have different flags but they are all the same. Look George I am not a clever man by no means but one thing that I have learnt, there are no white men and black men, or Christians and Jews or whatever, all there is rich people and poor people, and the rich people are all on the same side. They say they hate each other but it is all an act to fool us."

"No you're wrong," George pleaded, "listen Rod I owe you my life."

Rod looked at him coldly, "now I wish that I hadn't bothered. I am someone who sees a baby bird on the floor and picks the bird up and places it back in the nest, only for the baby bird to jump out again, no one is pushing you out George, you are jumping, there's no helping you George. Pray to God, because no one on earth can help you."

George looked at him, Rod maybe was the best man who he had ever met, but he never made him feel important as Chaval did, Chaval made him feel like he was part of some world wide network. "Join us Rod."

Rod shook his head, "no I was a slave once I ain't never going to be one again."

As they got nearer George stepped out and looked at the rope ladder, if he missed it he would sink down into the sea or maybe be hammered between the two vessels, "you can't want to stay on this little fishing boat."

"Better to be master of a little boat than a slave on a big one," Rod replied, "don't worry about me, I will find my way to Cherbourg alright. Good luck George."

George nodded, before leaping the five feet or so and grabbing the rope ladder before scaling slowly up it, Rod followed him only with his eyes: "You're going to need it."

Slowly George climbed up the ship's side before climbing over onto the ship's deck, as Rod swung the fishing boat sharp away and headed to where the lights of Cherbourg twinkled, he spoke no French, but what the hell, life was to be lived and he'd find another adventure somewhere.

Chaval offered out his hand with the broadest of grins, "amigo, but where is your friend, the tall man of the race of my ancestors?"

"He is a free spirit," George smiled.

"There is no room for individualism in the people's state," Chaval replied coldly, and looked at the little fishing boat and cursed that it was out of range of his cannons.

"So where are we heading for?"

'Kabinda," Chaval replied with a wisp in his smile, "the place where the earth oozes black with oil."

George nodded and looked into the darkness as Rod's boat disappeared and he wondered again if he had not done the wrong thing again. "What are we going to do there?"
"There will be a big meeting between all the old comrades, Fidel and Zedu will sit down, no doubt we will hear more stories of how they fought together against the terrorists of the black cockerels, and their racist white backers," Chaval smiled.

"It's funny, but I had a visitor in London, who was talking about things, he said that Kestrel had a number of Africans murdered, people from our own side, people who wanted to divide the country's wealth amongst the poor."

Chaval looked at him, "yes well he did."

George thought he must have misheard Chaval or maybe he was joking.

Chapter Ten:

Castle Hamlet was a different place with no George, and this time all knew that he would not be back, he had lead them up the hill only to lead them down again. Some of the leaders of the rebellion disappeared, went in to be questioned and were never seen again.

A few days later Jack Corn came to the hamlet, he was one of the characterless figures who orbited Prince Anthony, he was slightly dark due to his Canaanite ancestors. Few people knew what he stood for, save that he didn't like Arabian women veiling their faces, that was the only opinion he had had in forty years or more. He wouldn't have dared come if George would have still been there to argue with him, but without him Castle Hamlet was open to all of them. He stood on the village green and started talking. The crowd had never seen such a thing, and some thought it was a new type of travelling jester, who just wasn't funny, but maybe they weren't clever enough to get his jokes:

"It is of course a scandal that your representative is not in parliament speaking out for you. Look at the new carriageway they are building between London and Colchester, that could pass here! But without George there to argue for it it will go somewhere else."

"Good job too," all eyes turned to the hag as she walked forwards with one hand inside her knickers having a good scratch.

"Sorry Madame?"

"We don't want it! We don't want people coming here from Cold Chester, right proper bastards they are!"

Corn frowned, "but this place could change, it could be prosperous."

"Don't want Prospero!"

"There could be schools and hospitals," Corn gasped.

"Don't want them," the hag replied, "we don't want to learn what you want us to know. No one ever gets a job with what people teach them in your silly schools."

"What about the hospitals then," Corn pursued her, "what happens when you get ill?"

"When it's my time to die God will let us know, we don't need your quacks with their funny potions. When I was in Roach Chester once, there was some man who had hit his wife on the head with a mallet. I was going to run off to the peelers but some Vicar told me not to. He told me that the woman was sick and because there was no hospital in Roach Chester he had to treat her himself! The woman had got something called clay media."

"Chlamydia?" Corn replied, "that's not serious."

"It was for her, especially after she gave it to him!"

The crowd laughed, Corn frowned, "as I said before George should be arguing for Castle Hamlet."

"He never did that anyway, he was more interested in Arabians and Jews, them two can never get along, I use to live next to a couple like that, always arguing they were, until he killed her. Then it was a lot more peaceful, and I could get some sleep at night."

Corn leant forwards, "well I'm glad you raised that issue Madame, George didn't focus on local issues."

"Neither do you lot, your bloke is always on about Muscovy and Mesopo bloody tamia and places I don't know anything about, I mean all them places could sink to the bottom of the sea for all I care."

"I think we have done a good job in Mesopotamia," Corn tried to reply but the crowd booed him and Corn knew that they were still the same type of scum that they had always been.

"What that's got to do with me?" The hag retorted, "your boss is the Prime Minister of England not Mesopotamia!"

Slyface edged through the crowd and on the doors of Castle Hamlet itself next to the wanted poster for Dick Turpin he nailed one up for Lord Patrick Pantsdown 100 shillings was his price, then one which just said Rod 150 was his price. Lastly Slyface nailed up one for George Dumfries, his price was 25 shillings and it never said wanted.

Corn began to retreat as voices were raised, "you talk about free elections in Mesopotamia when are we going to get them here?"

"I don't want free elections," the hag argued, "if we choose our own prime minister we might choose the wrong one."

"We've got the wrong one already!" The blacksmith replied and so it went on in Castle Hamlet.

The days passed as George became more and more a person of memories, he was no Robin Hood or Hereward the Wake, he was a nobody, history quickly forgot him. As the ship made it's way down the Bay of Biscay George was already getting tiresome, as they past the Iberian peninsula, he was getting irritating, and as they passed the straits of Gibraltar and sighted the African coast Chaval was ready to slit him open and feed him to the sharks.

 Chaval was beginning to regret ever letting him on board. At first he was a little interested in what he had to say, but quickly all the stories of Prince Tony's secret killings wore thin. Chaval looked at him, not sure if he was serious or not. He would spit venom against Prince Tony and relate the story of Crook over and over again, what a scandal it was, each time he would add something extra. Then he would talk of Dr Keller, the man who had mysteriously slit his own wrists, and King Rat the leader of the pro-English death squads in the northern province, who had been executed in gaol. Chaval nodded, but in truth he could see little wrong with what he was being told, if Crook had fallen out with the leader he deserved to die. If King Rat was a trouble maker and Dr Keller couldn't keep his mouth shut then both deserved what they got as well. Chaval however was more perplexed when George spoke of Kestrel, it was as if he was in love with the man, his eyes shone like when a bible basher spoke of Jesus.

They were passing the place where the Gambian river poured into the sea, they had given it a wide birth because the British banner already fluttered from a fortress there. George was still speaking of Kestrel: "And you know he has not robbed one farthing from the people of Havana, not one."

Chaval smiled, "he has not stolen one farthing, no he has stolen the whole island!"

George stopped and looked at him, "sorry?"

"I have to face my people in an election every four years, Kestrel has not faced an election for forty years."

"But the people support him," Chaval argued.

"Who supports having the same leader for that long? However good he is, you want a change," Chaval sighed. "The man, the man who came to see you in London, the one who called himself Alves, he was telling the truth about everything save his name."

"But that can't be! Fidel Kestrel helped the people of Africa drive out the European slave masters!"

Chaval smiled, "I do not know if you believe what you say. I do not know what really happened back there in England, whether you were betrayed or if you betrayed them, if you are now betraying me." George was about to argue when Chaval held up his hand to silence him. "It's alright George, whatever the story is it's alright." He then drew back and the laughter died in his eyes, "there is a cemetery on the coast of Africa where to enter it is like entering the end of the earth. I went there once and as I entered the place I felt the force of a thousand murdered souls hit me. So many people had been killed so quickly that they had not had time to bury them properly and so arms and legs sprout from the earth. I could see skulls which bore machete marks. In other countries they would hide such things but there in Loanda they do not, neither does anyone have to lie about who did it, your friend Fidel Kestrel. Not personally of course, but his death squads went out there and did it."

"If that was the case then the colonists would keep on about it, so would the English," George argued.

"No one says anything because everyone are friends, the colonists, the English, the Muscovites, and they all supported what Kestrel did in that cursed African hell hole. The man who visited you was not called Alves because Alves is long dead, and he was no small man but a big man. Your visitor was using the name of a dead man. The real Alves saw power taken from the white men and then it return to them, the same faces came back, the same people who had worked for the Portuguese. He was no racist, his woman was white, he just wanted the people to have power of their own country, so Fidel had him killed, and not just him, but his woman and their baby, and his friends, and his comrades, and thousands of others." Chaval let his words sink in before he repeated, "thousands!"

"But why did Fidel do it?" George asked, half believing the story.

"The country was too rich to waste the money there, the hospitals, the libraries, the schools were needed back in Havana, and so the money was spent there, and the Africans only got war, massacres and servitude. Of course the Africans fought back, they rallied to a man called the Black Cockerel, and he came close to winning, but Kestrel sent so many men over they were outgunned four to one, and they lost in the end," Chaval smiled and held up his hands.

"That's not what you say outside, in your speeches," George retorted.

"We are all playing a double game," Chaval smiled, "how long do you think I would last out there if I told the truth?"

George drew back and waited for Chaval to smile, "you are jesting with me, this is all some jape."

"Jape?" Chaval repeated.

"Alright a test, you are testing me," George replied.

Chaval smiled, "I am not testing anyone, I am telling you this because since you have lost your *barrio,* your fiefdom as it was, you are a laird without a castle." The South American paused and smiled, proud of some of the words he had used.

"What do you mean?"

Chaval's eyes leveled on him, "you should be careful George, because you are no longer useful to us."

George drew back, maybe Rod had been right about this man, he had best talk little more before they reached Kabinda. He only had one more conversation before they reached Kabinda, it was as he walked along the deck one of the sailors hissed at him, "English are you?"

George looked at him, "sorry?"

"Are you English?" The man repeated.

George looked at him, "no, Scottish," he replied.

The sailor nodded, "that's good, then we are brothers, you see I am a Welshman."

"Are you?" George drew towards him, "how do you come to be in Chaval's navy then?"

"I am a Welshman but also a South American, you see there was a place in the Argentine that was Welsh, as Welsh as Harlech but it has all gone now."He smiled, "my father was one of the original settlers who left Wales, because they could see it becoming more and more English, they could see the old language dying slowly out. So to save our ways and our culture, to stop us becoming English we sailed south to the Argentine, there we would find some place where we could save Wales. The Argentines gave us a place no one wanted, there were no Europeans there, only natives. It was a wild and barren place, but you know we did it? We made a miracle. Together with the natives we built something out of nothing we irrigated the land, our people worked day and night, made it rich, built towns. Then do you know what happened?"

George shook his head, "no?"

"Then they came, the Spanish. wave after wave of them and they took it all from us, only the names of the towns are Welsh now, no one speaks it anymore, they all speak Spanish. Have you been to Wales my friend?" The sailor asked.

George nodded, "many times."

"What is it like?"

George smiled, "very beautiful."

The sailor nodded, "maybe one day I will see it, I hope so. There is no place in South America for Welsh people anymore." He then turned away and called out to someone in Spanish, George bet that no one on the ship knew he was Welsh. The Spanish, Portuguese and French could all have their colonies but the Welsh had been denied even one small part of Patagonia, they had travelled all that way simply to replace English serfdom for Spanish.

A month past before they looked out onto the coast of Africa, Chaval lowered his telescope, "there she is! Kabinda!"

George frowned, "but there is nothing there!"

"Nothing there!" Chaval mocked, "this is the land which kept the Portuguese empire afloat, this fed the bellies of it's soldiers and put the guns into their hands. Once all the Congo was in the hands of the Lusitanian throne, but they were too weak to keep it, and so the land north of Kabinda was taken by the French and the land to the east was taken by the Walloons and the Flemish, in their strange ungodly empire of madness. People laughed at the Portuguese reduced to this mere corner of what they had once had but this corner is the richest land on earth!" The ship sailed towards it, "the Kabindans fought for their freedom, and they still fight, but they will never get it"

"Why?"

"Because this land is too rich," Chaval repeated, "how can such riches be left in the hands of black Africans? Forty years ago Kestrel's ships came here, passing the

Portuguese ships leaving. The people were celebrating their freedom, they had a few hours of freedom before they passed from one empire to another. That is the way of the world my friend George. Maybe no one in the world is free, maybe freedom doesn't exist at all, anywhere."

The ship then sailed towards the harbor, there wasn't much to see here, the Portuguese had built little, and it had been scantly touched by the war, but above it in the jungle the sounds of cannon fire could still be heard. Chaval smiled, "they are on their own now the Kabindans, they will not last much longer."

George thought that maybe he should go and help them, but he didn't know what to think. As the ship came into moor, his eyes settled on a strange looking man, his face as dark as as the darkest African but his features narrow like a white man's. He stood there surrounded by a dozen men, and beyond that dozen, there was another dozen and another. "Who is that?"

"Zedu," Chaval replied, "the King of Loanda and the Prince of Kabinda, Kestrel gave him this land, just gave it to him, like it was an old shirt."

The gang plank had no sooner been extended than Zedu strode up onto the ship as if he owned it. Chaval moved to him and kissed his cheeks, "*camarada,* how are you?"

Zedu smiled weakly, "I am fine *amigo.*" The time of *camaradas* had longsince passed.

Chaval smiled, as Zedu's guards ran up to his side. "May I present to you the leader of the English resistance, George Dumfries." Chaval then seized him and pushed him towards Zedu.

The black Caligula looked at him and then smiled, "Mr Dumfires we are truly honoured to have a writer such as yourself here."

George blushed like a teenage girl, "you flatter me Sir."

"No!" Zedu roared, "I have read all your books!"

"Really?" George couldn't believe it.

"Yes they have amused me greatly," Zedu smiled, "especially the one about brother Fidel." Zedu then laughed and everyone around him laughed as well, although they had not read the book and did not know the joke. "I lived through those times and know that they were not as you wrote them, but those who write the history ultimately make it."

George bowed, but had it not been all based on fact what he had written about the life of Fidel Kestrel? "Yes of course Sir, you were on the front line against the racists."

Zedu paid him a sideways glance, not knowing if he was being mocked or not, "yes I was."

Night drew in over Kabinda and what passed for a city sank into darkness, but a palace glittered with it's lanterns. The people lived in shacks tied together with vines. As they journeyed towards the palace, George looked out from his carriage onto poverty, real poverty not what passed for it in England, the kind of poverty where you did not eat for days, that became weeks and then you died. Kabindans who come to England laughed at the rats, but there were no rats here because people ate them. George huddled up inside the carriage and crossed himself, worried in case the great sea of torture suddenly swept forwards and engulfed him, but he couldn't keep out the cries of misery which wailed over this place. Also there were small dark clouds which seemed to settle over places before moving off, "what are they?" George asked Chaval who sat opposite in the carriage.

"Our friends," Chaval smiled, "the mosquitos, they kill a lot of colonists and Europeans who come here, they are filled with malaria, to be bitten by one means weeks of fever and then death. Their bites don't seem to effect us so much though, while the Englishman is sick in bed our people are out there getting rich," there was a glint in his eye as he smiled.

Such was the misery and the grinding poverty that the splendour that they entered seemed like they were entering another world and George's jaw dropped. Fountains of the purest water gushed out contrasting sharply with the sewers of black on the other side of the walls.

Chaval looked with amusement at George's wonderment, "this is nothing compared with his palace in Loanda."

"Why does he do nothing to help the poor?" George asked.

"The poor will always be with us, as Jesus said," Chaval laughed.

Huge gates of iron spikes were drew back and they passed two lines of muskets, the guards bowing towards Zedu. "He is like a king," George gasped.

"He is more than a king," Chaval replied, "does your king in England have all this?"

George shook his head, and then gazed back into the slum.

Chaval laughed again, "they are the lucky ones my friend, in the provinces they are really poor, there is a grinding poverty there, because once the Portugues left everything collapsed, they are eating each other out there."

The palace had the longest veranda he had ever seen and stood outside the great pillared entrance was a face George knew from the journal sketches. "That is Edward Flanagan, what is he doing here?"

Chaval smiled and leant back, "this is Kabinda George everyone is here."

Zedu's carriage pulled up before Flanagan and he rushed forwards to take his hand and help him out of the carriage, "but they are the enemy!" George stammered.

Chaval's head tilted back in laughter, "this is Kabinda, it is a magical place everyone is friends here."

"But the Flanagan family tried to kill Fidel!" George argued.

"Oh that was a long time ago!" Chaval laughed."You have to live now not yesterday George."

"But they sent him a cigar which blew up!" George tried again.

Chaval laughed, "when was that? Not even in your father's day but your grandfather's day George, forget about it already!"

George drew back, he was even beginning to sound like a colonist.

Their carriage stopped George got out and walked to where Zedu and Flanagan still talked. Zedu jabbed his finger, "look I don't need no lectures off you, your family is getting rich out of Kabinda as well!"

"So are you!" Flanagan spat back.

"It's my country!" Zedu protested.

"Hardly," Flanagan smiled, "I know your story Zedu."

The black man then nodded, "there is a difference between you and I Flanagan. You live in one world, the world of business, I live in that world but I also live in a world of torture and death. Have you ever seen anyone tortured?"

Flanagan shook his head, "no."

"I have not just seen someone being tortured, I have done it myself," Zedu smiled.

"You can't scare me Zedu," Flanagan lied.

"Yes I can." Zedu replied.

George passed Flanagan and the colonist paid him glance, George smarted that he never recognized him. Beyond the walls maybe things were desperate but inside the palace there was no want for anything, it hardly looked like Africa, with lines of bottles of French wine and a huge pig turning on a spit. Everyone was here: British, colonists, French , German , Muscovites, Manchurians, Japanese and all types of Africans. Chaval lost himself in the crowd and was glad to have divorced himself from George. He wandered as if lost through the Babel of voices until he heard a voice behind him: "George Dumfries."

George turned and staggered back as he saw a face from a nightmare, it was him! The butcher! The same soul less eyes stared into his, and George thought he was going to die, but instead of a machete in his hand he held a plate of cold meat, instead of the ragged battle dress he wore a dinner suit, even a bow tie! He smiled, now he spoke English, "George it has been a long time."

George staggered back, his eyes fixed on the dead eyes, until the butcher finally turned and spoke to a man dressed in the flowing robes of an Arabian prince. George's head swirled, he kept looking back at the butcher, whose eyes shifted onto him as he talked to the prince, until Fidel arrived! There was no fanfare for the man who had made Zedu *rei*. He noticed his former mentor arrive but couldn't be bothered to walk over to greet him. However when George saw him he rushed over, it was him! The beard was now grey instead of black, but it was him. "Fidel! Fidel!" Kestrel looked about and staggered back as George headed towards him, seizing his hand and kissing it.

Fidel tried to wriggle away, "who is this idiot?"

Chaval moved forwards, "this is the British parliamentarian George Dumfries?"

"What my propaganda man?" Fidel frowned, "but he seems like a crazy man."

"It has long been my dream to meet the leader of the world rebellion!" George kissed his hand again.

Kestrel looked at Chaval who just smiled, and shrugged.

Zedu had at last made it over to welcome the *commandante*, "oh Fidel, to what do we owe the honour?" He mocked.

"Just to see that our friends don't forget about us," Kestrel replied acidly, "forget about the sacrifices we made for victory."

"Of course not," Zedu smiled.

"Without us the Black Cockerel would have won," Fidel reminded him.

"I see you have a new dog," Zedu nodded towards George still slobbering over Kestrel's hand. Kestrel yanked his hand away from him and entered the party with his back straight.

Zedu then turned to one of his aides, "who keeps inviting that old fool?"

"You owe him," Chaval reminded him.

"Not really, he only sent soldiers over here because the Muscovites ordered him to, he wouldn't have done otherwise, he doesn't give a damn about black people. He's just an old bastard, coming up here, trying to spoil my party," Zedu moaned.

Chaval smiled and slid his arm around his waist, "come on brother let's get some food."

The top table was the longest table George had ever seen with Zedu sat in the middle surrounded by his family and his wife's family, otherwise known as the government. The butcher was there, only four seats away from Zedu, was George the only person who knew who he was? George was sat on one of the lesser tables, behind a pillar. Kestrel at least was on the main table but at the far end, but his voice made it to Zedu, "of course he'd hanging from a Bakongo noose now if it wasn't for me, I saved them." Zedu glanced down the table at him and a flash of anger swept his face. Kestrel though carried on, "now he doesn't want anything to do with me, look at him talking to that imperialist bastard!"

The butcher got to his feet, and whispered something to Zedu. Zedu smiled and shook his head, before the butcher sat down again.

Fidel spoke then louder, "nobody wanted him to be the president, there was someone before him, we killed him for you."

Zedu smiled again, and looked embarrassed.

Fidel continued, "he's no more African than I am, just because he is black doesn't make him African!"

Zedu then lost his cool, "you are the imperialist Fidel! No one invited you here! You started the war! Without you there would have been an election, maybe we would have lost, maybe not. If we would have lost then we would have worked with the others, that is the way civilized countries are, but you wouldn't let us be civilized. You ruined this country Fidel not me, the problem was there before I ever got into power! Because the man you put in power was a madman! He could only work with foreigners not his own people!You are a world wide bandit, you talk of me but you yourself are not from Havana, your parents were Galicians, beggars who went to the Caribbean to loot it, you are no better than anyone else here. You are an imperialist who is the son of imperialists!"

Fidel had never been spoken to like that, and he got to his feet clutching his heart, he moved his mouth but nothing came out, then from one of the lesser tables a broad Scottish accent came: "That's not true!" George got to his feet. "This man is a true fighter for the rights of others, he has dedicated his life to the poor and down trodden, in bringing justice to the world! He is a beacon to thousands, nay millions across the world!" George then looked over the tables, all were serious then Flanagan sniggered, and Zedu caught it and then the whole room joined in, even Kestrel was laughing in the end.

"Who is this guy?" Zedu dried the tears of laughter from his eyes.

"It's George Dumfries!" Chaval replied, he then called out, "sit down George you've given us all a good laugh already!"

As George sat down he felt a hand on his shoulder, he turned round, and he heard an English accent. "George, that was a good one, I am the British ambassador, do you have anywhere to stay?"

"No."

"Well stay at the embassy then."

"But I am a wanted man," George argued.

"Wanted by whom?"

"Nobody," George admitted.

The End.

I dedicate this novel to the memory of my grandfather Victor Fowler, someone I loved greatly and still do.

Also to the memory of my father in law Joao Manuel Felicio, and to all those who cherish the idea of the total independence of nations.

By the same author:

The Three Wise Demon Killers

Dr Jekyll and Comrade Hyde

Vampire Mercenary

The Last Lord of Holt Castle

All available on Amazon